AF679188

THE AUTISM GUIDE FOR ADULTS

INSIGHTS FOR SELF-DISCOVERY, IDENTITY, PERSONAL GROWTH, SOCIAL CONNECTION, PROFESSIONAL DEVELOPMENT AND HOW TO ACHIEVE YOUR SUCESS BEYOND LABELS

JJ Andrade, MBA

THE AUTISM GUIDE FOR ADULTS

INSIGHTS FOR SELF-DISCOVERY, IDENTITY, PERSONAL GROWTH, SOCIAL CONNECTION, PROFESSIONAL DEVELOPMENT AND HOW TO ACHIEVE YOUR SUCCESS BEYOND LABELS

To Daniel Andrade,

I hope this book serves as a lasting reminder of courage, purpose, and authenticity. You are the shining light in my life, and I encourage you to embrace the beauty of being your authentic self as you grow. Thank you for helping me discover my own path with confidence, reminding me that my story matters, and that our possibilities are limitless.

With all my love,

Dad

© Copyright JJ Andrade 2025 - All rights reserved.

The content within this book may not be reproduced, duplicated or transmitted without direct written permission from the author or the publisher.

Under no circumstances will any blame or legal responsibility be held against the publisher or author, for any damages, reparation, or monetary loss due to the information contained within this book. Either directly or indirectly. You are responsible for your own choices, actions, and results.

Legal Notice:

This book is copyright protected. This book is only for personal use. You cannot amend, distribute, sell, use, quote or paraphrase any part, of the content within this book, without the consent of the author or publisher.

Disclaimer Notice:

Please note the information contained within this document is for educational and entertainment purposes only. All effort has been expended to present accurate, up-to-date, and reliable, complete information. No warranties of any kind are declared or implied. Readers acknowledge that the author is not engaging in the rendering of legal, financial, medical or professional advice. The content within this book has been derived from various sources. Please consult a licensed professional before attempting any techniques outlined in this book.

By reading this document, the reader agrees that under no circumstances is the author responsible for any losses, direct or indirect, which are incurred as a result of the use of the information contained within this document, including, but not limited to, — errors, omissions, or inaccuracies.

Introduction

There was a reasonably uneventful moment in its setup, yet severe in its impact. Sitting across from a psychotherapist, I received words that would forever change how I saw myself: "You are gifted and have Level 1 ASD (Autism Spectrum Disorder)." In that instant, my world seemed to pause, and a flood of clarity washed over me. What had felt like a lifetime of peculiarities and moments of not fitting in suddenly made sense.

It was as if a veil had been lifted, revealing an intricate tapestry of experiences that shaped who I am. Receiving my diagnosis of Level 1 ASD and giftedness as an adult felt like finding a map after wandering lost in a maze for years. It was both liberating and overwhelming—liberating because it offered a framework to understand past struggles and victories, and overwhelming because it demanded a reexamination of my identity and the courage to embrace it.

This revelation turned confusion into understanding, empowering me to reclaim my narrative with newfound confidence. For years, I had lived in a world of imitation, striving to conform to social norms that never quite made sense. Social interactions felt like puzzles with missing pieces, and unwritten rules eluded my grasp. I navigated life by mimicking behaviors and deciphering social cues as if they were in a foreign language. Despite my best efforts, I often felt like an actor on stage, delivering lines that never seemed entirely right. I attributed much of this social dissonance to being from another culture. However, after my diagnosis, I embarked on a journey of transformation and acceptance, learning to recognize my authentic self and celebrate the unique ways my mind works.

I am JJ Andrade—not a psychotherapist or certified ASD specialist—but someone who was born on this path and emerged with a deeper understanding of what it means to be autistic in a world built for neurotypicals. My professional background spans data science, business management, engineering, and disciplines that may seem unrelated at first glance but are intricately connected by a shared pursuit of efficiency and purpose. This guide draws from those fields, blending insights from psychology, Christian principles, and Stoic virtues to offer a holistic approach to self-discovery and personal growth.

This book is more than just a guide; it's a companion on our shared journey toward understanding and empowerment. Unlike academic textbooks, this guide focuses on practical, actionable strategies for self-advocacy, personal growth, and professional success—delivered by someone with 'skin in the game'. It promotes the understanding and acceptance of neurodiversity, encouraging readers to embrace their unique strengths and identities.

This resource aims to help readers overcome common challenges faced by autistic adults, such as navigating social interactions, advancing in their careers, and exploring personal identity. Its intended audience includes autistic adults seeking empowerment, neurodivergent individuals embracing their identity, personal development enthusiasts, and advocates of autism awareness. The guide acknowledges the diverse backgrounds and needs of its readers, offering a strengths-based approach tailored to a culturally rich audience.

The framework of The Autism Guide for Adults is modeled after the structure of a sacred text, divided into 4 distinct books, each with a thematic focus: The Book of Identity and Self-Confidence; The Book of Social Skills and Relationships; The Book of Professional Career Growth; and The Book of Continuous Improvement and Lifelong Success.

Each book delves deeply into these themes, providing a comprehensive foundation for personal development. What distinguishes this guide is its focus on practical strategies and my real-life experiences offering insights and my neurodivergent lens on these topics, empowering readers to explore their potential and achieve their goals.

While I share my personal journey, I fully acknowledge that Level 1 ASD (commonly referred to as Asperger's) is much broader than my individual experience. As you engage with this book, I encourage you to actively reflect on the content, apply the strategies, and share your experiences with your community—including those at higher levels of the spectrum. This guide invites you to embark on a path of self-discovery and empowerment, offering a roadmap to navigate life beyond labels and thrive. Could this be the spark that helps you redefine success in your own unique way?

Book 1: The Book of Identity and Self-Confidence

Have you ever experienced a discovery so extensive that it urges you to take another look at every element of your presence? For lots of adult autistics, getting a medical diagnosis later on in life is precisely such a discovery, a critical minute that changes complications right into clearness. It is an unknotting of kinds, a discovery brightening the detailed patterns and actions that had formerly appeared mysterious. Truthfully, this medical diagnosis usually functions as a sign, assisting one with the puzzle of past experiences and allowing a fresh understanding of one's identification.

You are handed a key to a door that has been secured for several years. Behind it, there exists a wide range of self-awareness and perspective.

1.1 Discovering Your Neurodiversity: A Journey to Late Diagnosis

Comprehending Late Diagnosis is both a powerful and also transformative experience. For those who have actually browsed the complexities of life without the advantage of this understanding, the discovery of an autism medical diagnosis in their adult years can be a transitional phase.

It brings an extensive feeling of alleviation as the challenge items of one's life ultimately mesh perfectly.

You are no longer limited to questioning why social interactions felt difficult or why specific environments seemed frustrating. This newfound clarity provides a perspective that allows you to reframe your experiences, transforming past struggles into stories of resilience and strength. You start to see the one-of-a-kind strength that has constantly belonged to your identification, currently contextualized with the lens of neurodiversity.

Browsing the psychological reactions to a late medical diagnosis is a trip in itself, rife with a range of feelings varying from alleviation to complication and also eventually approval. It is all natural to feel a pooling of these sensations as you are concerned about the redefinition of your self-identity. Some people locate relief in the recognition that includes comprehending why they have constantly felt various, while others might rush with the ramifications of their medical diagnosis. You could experience minutes of contemplation examining the social standards you when made every effort to mimic.

To refine these feelings efficiently, consider embracing mindfulness and reflective journaling techniques.

These devices can help you share your ideas and feelings, supplying a refuge to discover your progressing identity.

Constructing a brand-new self-understanding requires representation and intentionality. As you reframe your past thoughts, emotions, and actions through the lens of autism, you might find yourself reassessing your strengths and weaknesses.

This reevaluation is not just a workout in self-contemplation but also an effective way of self-discovery and development. Journaling workouts can be essential, enabling you to record your ideas and sensations as they progress. Think about covering specific experiences that soon mystified you, and also check out how your brand-new understanding of autism gives clearness. You might locate that the top qualities you, as soon as viewed as weak points, are strengths that can be leveraged to your benefit.

In this phase, we will discover how to grow a durable understanding of your identity, supplying understandings and methods to encourage you to accept your genuine self. As you start this transformative trip, remember you are not the only one.

Numerous others have walked this course and discovered strength in their neurodiversity, finding that the top qualities that set them apart are the actual attributes that make them remarkable. Welcome this trip with inquisitiveness and an open heart, prepared to discover the midsts of your capacity and the wealth of your identity.

1.2 Welcoming Your Special Identification in a Neurotypical World

Living in a society that adheres to neurotypical standards presents a unique set of challenges, especially when it comes to maintaining authenticity. From a young age, we are subtly conditioned to conform to societal expectations, prioritizing conformity over individuality. This pressure to assimilate can feel like an invisible burden, pushing us to reshape ourselves into forms that don't quite fit.

Envision a sculptor sculpting at a block of marble, not to disclose the inborn charm within yet to require it right into a fixed type. The social assumption to adjust can be as stiff as the carver's sculpt, plus the battle to stay genuine despite this stress can be difficult. A single thing needs to initially acknowledge these assumptions of what they are, which does not specify your actual worth or possibility. Recognizing and examining these standards is necessary to remain authentic, permitting you to sculpt your course with intention and stability.

Remaining faithful to oneself requires a commitment to self-awareness and self-questioning. It's about recognizing and embracing the unique traits and perspectives that set you apart. This means acknowledging your strengths, such as heightened attention to detail or perceiving patterns others might overlook.

It includes identifying and welcoming the distinct characteristics and viewpoints that set you apart. This indicates recognizing your strengths, such as a heightened focus on information or the capability to regard patterns others could ignore.

These are not flaws to be hidden but rather aspects of your identity that deserve celebration. Staying true to yourself requires a conscious decision to resist societal pressure to conceal or downplay your neurodiversity. It involves cultivating a sense of self-respect independent of external validation and finding solace in the knowledge that authenticity is a strength, not a weakness.

Commending neurodiversity is an act of disobedience versus the extensive idea that distinction corresponds to shortage.

It celebrates the range of human experience and recommends that variety improves our world. Welcome favorable self-affirmations that enhance your worth and possibilities. Advise yourself daily that your neurodiversity is not a barrier but a distinct lens through which you see the world, supplying valuable and essential viewpoints.

Take into consideration the tales of effective autistic people who have not just accepted their neurodiversity yet have actually prospered as a result of it.

Consider trendsetters like Temple Grandin, whose insights into pet actions have transformed animal handling, or Greta Thunberg, whose unrelenting dedication to ecological advocacy has galvanized an international movement. These people function as effective reminders that neurodiversity is not something to be camouflaged but something to be commemorated and shared.

Structured self-esteem in a world that typically misinterprets or weakens neurodiversity entails an intentional initiative to cultivate a favorable self-image. Confidence-building workouts can be an efficient means of improving positive self-image.

Participate in tasks highlighting your toughness, whether innovative searches, problem-solving obstacles, or public talking possibilities. Role-play situations can additionally be an essential tool in browsing social communications, enabling you to exercise and fine-tune your interaction abilities in a secure and encouraging atmosphere.

These workouts offer not only the method but also the peace of mind that you can browse social contexts with grace and self-confidence.

As you accept your unique identification, remember that credibility is not a location but a constant method.

It is the determination to back your worth together with realities and when they deviate from the standard. In doing so, you led the way for others to comply with developing a culture that deserves variety in all its types. Welcome your neurodiversity with satisfaction and allow it to assist you, for it is your most significant possession, a testimony to your durability and possibility.

1.3 Breaking Stereotypes: Redefining Autism Beyond Labels

Stereotypes about autism often perpetuate misconceptions that reduce the diverse range of neurodivergent experiences to simplistic caricatures. These misconceptions can range from the assumption that all autistic individuals are mathematical geniuses in the Hollywood mold to the belief that autism is synonymous with a lack of empathy or social interest. Such stereotypes not only obscure the diversity within the autism spectrum but also foster misunderstanding and stigma. It's crucial to challenge these stereotypes and promote open discussions that debunk biased beliefs and encourage a more inclusive understanding of autism.

The fact is even more refined as each person's experience of autism is unique and formed by individual, ecological together, and social variables.

For example, while some people might undoubtedly stand out in details, others may not fit these slim meanings yet have toughness in creative thinking, analytical, or psychological knowledge. Enlightening peers and coworkers is crucial in dismantling these misunderstandings, welcoming open discussions that test prejudiced ideas, and promoting a much more comprehensive understanding of autism.

To redefine individual identification past public tags, people must craft a story that resonates with their genuine selves. This entails mindful separation from the tags imposed by outside assumptions, welcoming a self-definition that mirrors lived experiences and individual worth.

One reliable approach is to compose an individual's required statement of ideas, strengths, and ambitions. This paper is a practical suggestion of the originality and uniqueness that define everyone, providing clarity and conviction despite the social stress of adjustment.

Sharing individual tales and experiences can be transformative for the narrator and the target market. These stories confirm individual identification and influence others to see past the tags, acknowledging the deepness and intricacy of autistic experiences.

Favorable depiction in media coupled with culture plays a vital function in forming public assumptions and understanding autism. It is essential to highlight varied autistic examples throughout numerous areas, from professional athletes to stars, researchers, and lobbyists. These people oppose fashions, showcasing the diverse nature of autism and also the capacity for success in various domain names. For example, the success of people like Sir Anthony Hopkins, who has actually openly reviewed his autism, shows that neurodiversity can accompany imaginative greatness and also praise.

Promoting precise media representations is just as vital as ensuring that the stories about autism reflect its variety and depth. A depiction that adequately captures the range of autistic experiences can dissipate misconceptions and urge approval, paving the way for a much more comprehensive culture.

Creating environments where open dialogue about autism can flourish is crucial. These spaces foster understanding and empathy, allowing individuals to share their experiences and insights without fear of judgment or misunderstanding. We can break down barriers, dispel myths, and foster a more inclusive society by promoting open discussions.

Holding or joining panel conversations offers a system for varied voices within the autistic neighborhood to be listened to, cultivating discussion that tests stereotypes and advertises recognition. Social media sites additionally provide an effective method for producing recognition, offering a discussion forum for people to share their tales and supporters for adjustment and connecting with an international area. We can use these systems to enhance traditionally marginalized voices, adding to a broader social change in inclusivity and understanding.

As we browse these complicated motifs, we must approach them with compassion and an eagerness to test our presumptions.

By damaging fashions and redefining autism past tags, we not only recognize previous thoughts, emotions, and actions related to autism but likewise contribute to a cumulative story that commemorates neurodiversity as an essential component of the human experience.

Let us aim to develop a world where everyone is attended to their distinct payments and possibilities without the restrictions of outdated tags and assumptions.

1.4 The Power of Self-Advocacy: Your Voice, Your Strength

Self-advocacy is a cornerstone of empowerment, especially for autistic people browsing a world that frequently misunderstands or neglects their needs. It includes expressing one's wishes and choices and civil liberties, safeguarding essential lodgings in different contexts, whether in the office, academic setups, or individual connections. For numerous people, this idea might initially appear complicated; however, it is critical to comprehend that self-advocacy does not almost require what is required; it concerns growing a feeling of company and freedom.

The abilities called for consist of positive interaction, self-awareness, and an understanding of one's civil liberties and readily available sources. Positive includes revealing oneself truthfully and considerately, without hostility or passivity, an equilibrium that frequently needs technique and self-confidence.

Navigating organizations and systems requires a clear understanding of their structures, which can frequently be complicated and frightening. Yet, understanding how to connect your requirements properly can turn these communications into opportunities for development and assistance.

Interaction abilities are essential to self-advocacy, functioning like the automobile, where one's voice is listened to.

Assessing previous experiences and comparing minutes of genuine interaction with minutes of a replica of social standards is simple. Many autistic people, myself included, have actually invested years resembling actions to harmonize commonly at the expense of credibility. Nevertheless, reliable self-advocacy requires authentic expression. Exercising assertiveness can start with tiny actions such as sharing choices in low-stakes circumstances or utilizing "I" declarations to communicate sensations and requirements plainly.

In addition, aesthetic help coupled with devices such as graphs or composed notes can be instrumental in promoting interaction, especially in settings where singing expression can be tested.

These assistances are a bridge, ensuring one's message is shared precisely and thoroughly.

Producing an individual campaigning strategy is a calculated effort that encourages people to come close to self-advocacy with objective and quality. This strategy entails laying out particular campaigning for objectives, determining the locations where assistance is required, and mapping out the actions needed to attain these objectives.

Consider what holiday accommodations or modifications would substantially improve your lifestyle or workplace, and focus on these in your strategy. In addition, it is necessary to determine allies coupled with sources that can sustain your campaigning for initiatives. Allies could consist of relied-on coworkers, coaches, or participants of the neurodivergent area that recognize plus sustain your requirements. Constructing a network of assistance reinforces your campaigning for initiatives and supplies motivation and assistance when obstacles emerge.

Eliminating campaigning for difficulties is an unpreventable component of the procedure, as resistance and troubles prevail. Building durability when confronted with these barriers is necessary, enabling you to navigate them with determination and flexibility.

One technique is to reframe problems as discovering experiences that can improve your method and enhance your resolve. Strength is cultivated with determination and the determination to adjust methods as required, identifying that each difficulty is a possibility to expand and boost your campaigning abilities.

Despite how little these triumphs suggest your capacities and progression, it is essential to commemorate successes.

In the world of self-advocacy, your voice is your strength, an effective device that, when persuaded efficiently, can change your experience and communication skills. The trip towards efficient self-advocacy is just one of continual development, plus knowing that every action taken is a testimony to your durability and resolution. Accept this procedure with self-confidence and inquisitiveness, recognizing that your voice issues and campaigning for initiatives add to a broader motion towards addition and understanding.

As you progress on this journey, please remember that self-advocacy does not practically accomplish particular results; it is about living a life where your needs are acknowledged and valued.

1.5 Commemorating Toughness: Transforming Difficulties into Success

In the substantial tapestry of human experience, each string stands for a unique toughness, skill, or skill that adds to the abundant variety of life. For those on the autism spectrum, determining and commemorating these strings can transform obstacles into successes.

The initial step in this transformative procedure is identifying your distinct toughness. Consider producing a strength inventory —a thorough listing incorporating your capabilities, abilities, and interests. Consider minutes when you have succeeded, whether in professional settings, individual jobs, or social communications. This workout highlights your skills and supplies a structure to construct your personal and professional life.

Participating in reflective exercises for self-awareness can brighten these challenges even more, providing an understanding of how they can be leveraged in numerous contexts.

While commonly complicated, obstacles hold the capacity for development and possibility. By reframing obstacles as possibilities, we cultivate a way of thinking that welcomes misfortune as a stimulant for growth.

Establishing analytic abilities is similar to developing a craft; each obstacle offers a brand-new challenge to address, a workout in resourcefulness and imagination.

Assess historical numbers and contemporaries that have transformed misfortune into benefit, utilizing their experiences to sustain advancement and success. From developers who have changed failings into innovative explorations to musicians who have used individual battles to develop engaging artworks, these studies are practical suggestions for human durability. Such tales influence us to watch each barrier as an action toward better success.

The growth of a development state of mind is essential in this search for continual growth.

This state of mind, identified by the idea that capabilities and knowledge can be created with commitment and effort, fosters durability and a love of understanding. Participate in mindset-shifting workouts that address concepts of capacity and capacity. For example, when confronted with a setback, the technique reframes the experience as a knowing possibility instead of a failure.

This change in point of view can change your technique to difficulties motivating determination along with technology.

Success tales abound of people who have accepted this mindset to accomplish exceptional development. These stories testify to the power of perseverance and the unlimited possibility that exists within everyone.

As you navigate your course, consider how your development and accomplishments can influence others within your neighborhood. Sharing success tales openly commemorates individual success and supplies hope and inspiration to others encountering comparable difficulties.

Whether through writing, talking engagements, or social media site systems, your tale can impact adjustment and promote understanding. In addition, it should consider the influence of mentoring and sustaining peers who are on comparable trips. You add to a society of permission and area assistance by supplying support, motivation, and learning. This mutual exchange of expertise and experience improves the advisor and the mentee, cultivating a feeling of link and shared objective.

In this interconnected world, the act of commemorating strengths prolongs past-specific empowerment. It adds to the cumulative story of human experience, improving the lives of those around us. Each difficulty was eliminated, each toughness commemorated, and each tale shared included a vibrant string to this story, advising us of the strength and perspective intrinsic to the human spirit. As you continue to discover and commemorate your one-of-a-kind toughness, recognize that you are not just changing your life but motivating others to identify and welcome their possibility.

1.6 Building Emotional Resilience: Tools for Mental Health

In the tapestry of human emotions, resilience stands out as a formidable thread, weaving strength and adaptability through the fabric of our day-to-day existence. Emotional resilience is not merely the ability to withstand life's adversities; it is an intricate dance of recovery and growth, a dynamic process that allows individuals to navigate the vicissitudes of life with equanimity and fortitude. This resilience is characterized by several key attributes, including optimism, flexibility, and the ability to maintain control under pressure. It is the quiet assurance that, despite the storms of uncertainty and change, one possesses the inner resources to weather them. In daily life, resilience confers myriad benefits, such as improved problem-solving abilities, enhanced emotional regulation, and a greater capacity for empathy and connection. By cultivating resilience, one bolsters their mental health and enriches their interactions with the world around them.

To foster emotional resilience, one must equip oneself with a toolkit of coping strategies tailored to manage stress and emotional challenges. Mindfulness and meditation serve as foundational elements in this toolkit, offering a refuge of calm amidst the chaos of modern life. Mindfulness, the practice of cultivating present-moment awareness, invites individuals to observe their thoughts and emotions without judgment, fostering clarity and acceptance. Meditation, whether through guided sessions or simple breathing exercises, provides a structured space for relaxation and introspection, helping to quiet the mind and reduce stress. Complementing these practices are cognitive-behavioral techniques, which empower individuals to identify and challenge negative thought patterns, transforming them into more constructive and realistic perspectives. By incorporating these strategies into daily routines, individuals can enhance their emotional resilience, building a robust framework for mental well-being.

The role of support systems in fostering resilience cannot be overstated. These networks of understanding and empathy provide a vital buffer against the stresses and strains of life, offering solace and encouragement when needed most. Identifying key support figures—family members, friends, or mentors—lays the foundation for a personal support network that can be relied upon in times of need. This network is not static but dynamic, evolving as relationships deepen and new connections are forged. Creating a personal support network involves nurturing these relationships with care and intention, prioritizing open communication and mutual understanding. By surrounding oneself with individuals who offer genuine support and encouragement, one can cultivate a sense of belonging and security, reinforcing the emotional resilience needed to navigate life's challenges.

Promoting mental well-being is a holistic endeavor encompassing self-care and professional support. Daily self-care routines are the bedrock of mental health, providing the structure and stability necessary for maintaining balance. These routines include exercise, healthy eating, and adequate sleep, all contributing to physical and emotional well-being. Engaging in hobbies and creative pursuits can also foster a sense of fulfillment and purpose, offering an outlet for self-expression and relaxation. In addition to personal practices, accessing professional mental health services is crucial to maintaining mental well-being. Therapists and counselors provide a safe space for exploring one's thoughts and emotions, offering guidance and support tailored to individual needs. Whether through in-person sessions or teletherapy options, professional support can be invaluable for those seeking to enhance their emotional resilience and overall mental health.

1.7 Understanding Mental Health in the Autistic Experience

The landscape of mental health within the autistic experience is a complex and nuanced tapestry, often characterized by unique challenges that diverge significantly from those faced by neurotypical individuals. Autism, with its myriad manifestations, intersects with mental health in ways that can amplify both anxiety and depression, conditions already prevalent in the general population but particularly pronounced within the autistic community. This heightened prevalence often stems from the sensory sensitivities and social dynamics inherent in autism, where environments perceived as neutral by neurotypicals can become overwhelming, leading to heightened stress and anxiety. Social isolation, a frequent companion for many autistic individuals, further exacerbates these mental health challenges, creating a vicious cycle of loneliness and emotional distress that can be difficult to break. The impact of feeling disconnected from peers, combined with the struggle to navigate often baffling social norms, can lead to a sense of alienation, compounding mental health difficulties.

The intersection between autism and mental health issues often presents a labyrinthine puzzle, where overlapping symptoms can blur diagnostic clarity. For instance, repetitive behaviors or intense focus, characteristic of autism, may be mistaken for symptoms of anxiety or obsessive-compulsive disorder, leading to potential misdiagnoses. Similarly, sensory processing issues, a common feature in autism, can significantly influence mental health, as the constant bombardment of sensory stimuli can lead to heightened anxiety or even panic attacks. Understanding these intersections is crucial, as it allows for a more nuanced approach to mental health care, one that acknowledges the unique ways in which autism and mental health conditions can interplay and exacerbate each other. Recognizing these intersections can pave the way for more tailored interventions, ensuring that the distinct needs of autistic individuals are met with empathy and precision.

Identifying signs and symptoms of mental health issues in autistic individuals requires a vigilant and nuanced approach, as these signs may manifest differently than in the neurotypical population. Changes in behavior or mood, such as increased irritability or withdrawal from social interactions, can be indicative of underlying mental health concerns. An autistic individual may begin to avoid activities they once enjoyed or exhibit changes in appetite and sleep patterns, subtle signals that something may be amiss. While often subtle, these changes can speak volumes about an individual's mental state, serving as crucial indicators that professional support may be needed. Careful observation and open communication are key in identifying these signs, enabling timely intervention and support.

Addressing the challenges of misdiagnosis and stigma in mental health care for autistic individuals is a matter of both advocacy and education. Common misdiagnoses, such as attributing sensory sensitivities to anxiety disorders or mistaking social withdrawal for depression without considering the context of autism, can lead to inappropriate treatment plans that do not address the root causes of distress. Advocacy for accurate diagnoses involves equipping oneself with knowledge about autism and its intersections with mental health, enabling more informed discussions with healthcare providers. Strategies for advocating for accurate diagnoses include seeking out professionals who specialize in autism and mental health, as well as utilizing resources such as the Autistic Self Advocacy Network, which provides guidance on navigating these complex healthcare landscapes. Additionally, fostering open dialogue about autism and mental health can help dismantle the stigma that often surrounds these topics, creating a more inclusive and understanding environment for all individuals.

1.8 Coping Mechanisms for Stress and Anxiety: Practical Approaches

Navigating stress and anxiety can feel like standing in a torrential downpour without an umbrella or shelter in sight. Recognizing the triggers and symptoms specific to your experience is crucial, akin to identifying the tell-tale signs of an impending storm. For many autistic individuals, stressors may include sensory overload, social interactions, or unexpected changes in routine. The physical manifestations of anxiety—racing heart, clammy hands, or that sinking feeling in your stomach—serve as important signals. To track these, consider keeping a journal where you document daily thoughts, emotions, and actions, noting recurring patterns. This can illuminate specific triggers, offering insight into how best to manage them. By reflecting on these entries, you'll better understand what exacerbates your stress and how your body responds, paving the way for more targeted coping strategies.

Developing personalized coping strategies is a craft that requires both creativity and introspection. Breathing exercises, such as the 4-7-8 technique, can provide immediate relief by slowing your heart rate and calming your nervous system. Visualization techniques are another potent tool; imagine a place where you feel completely at peace, whether a serene beach or a quiet forest. Picture every detail vividly—the sound of waves or the rustling of leaves—and let these images transport you to a calm state. These practices allow you to create a mental sanctuary where stress cannot intrude, providing a respite whenever needed. Experiment with different methods, tailoring them to suit your preferences, and don't hesitate to combine techniques for maximum efficacy.

Incorporating mindfulness practices into your routine can be a bulwark against stress and anxiety. Mindfulness invites you to engage fully with the present moment, observing thoughts and feelings without judgment. Guided meditation, for instance, can guide you through a journey of relaxation, helping to quiet the mental chatter that often accompanies stress. Mindful breathing exercises, where you focus solely on the rhythm of your breath, can anchor you in moments of turbulence, promoting a sense of stability and peace. These practices foster a deep understanding of awareness, allowing you to respond to stress with intention rather than reaction. Over time, mindfulness becomes a way of being, infusing daily life with tranquility and clarity.

Building a routine for stress management is akin to constructing a sturdy vessel capable of weathering any storm. Start by scheduling regular relaxation time, treating it as sacred and non-negotiable. This could be a daily walk in nature, a half-hour reading, or a warm bath—whatever soothes your soul and replenishes your spirit. Setting boundaries is equally important to prevent burnout; learn to avoid commitments that overextend you and prioritize activities that nourish your well-being. Establishing a routine reduces stress and enhances resilience, providing the structure and predictability many autistic individuals find comforting. This proactive approach to stress management ensures that when challenges arise, you are equipped to endure and thrive amidst adversity. As you integrate these practices into your life, remember that the goal is not to eliminate stress entirely—an impossible feat—but to cultivate the skills needed to navigate it gracefully and confidently.

1.9 Sensory Overload: Strategies for Regulation and Comfort

Sensory overload, for many autistic individuals, is akin to a cacophony of stimuli that overwhelms the senses, leaving one feeling trapped in a whirlwind of chaos. Imagine walking into a bustling subway station during rush hour: the blaring announcements, the jostling of hurried commuters, the blinding fluorescent lights—all converging into an inescapable storm. For autistic individuals, such sensory experiences can trigger an intense physiological response characterized by heightened anxiety, irritability, or even physical discomfort. This response is often a result of the brain's difficulty in filtering and processing incoming sensory information, leading to a sense of being bombarded by stimuli that others might perceive as merely background noise. Common environmental triggers for sensory overload include loud noises, bright lights, crowded spaces, and certain textures or smells, which can evoke a visceral, overwhelming, and exhausting reaction.

Creating a sensory-friendly environment is crucial in mitigating the risk of sensory overload, offering a sanctuary where one can find solace and clarity amidst the sensory chaos. Strategies for crafting such environments are varied, yet each is designed to minimize exposure to overwhelming stimuli. Noise-canceling headphones, for instance, can be a valuable tool in noisy spaces such as offices, public transport, or crowded events, providing a buffer against intrusive sounds and allowing for a sense of calm and focus. Designing a sensory-friendly workspace involves consideration of lighting, seating arrangements, and even color schemes—opt for soft, natural lighting, comfortable and supportive seating, and calming colors to create an atmosphere conducive to concentration and relaxation. Though seemingly minor, these adjustments can significantly enhance one's ability to function and thrive in environments that might otherwise provoke sensory overload.

When sensory overload strikes, having a repertoire of sensory regulation techniques can provide much-needed relief, allowing for a return to equilibrium. Deep pressure techniques, such as using a weighted blanket or engaging in firm hugs, can offer a soothing, grounding sensation that calms an overactive nervous system. Sensory breaks, short periods of respite from stimuli, can also be beneficial, providing an opportunity to regroup and recharge. These breaks involve stepping outside for fresh air, retreating to a quiet room, or engaging in calming activities such as music or guided meditation. By incorporating these techniques into daily routines, one can effectively manage and mitigate the impact of sensory overload, fostering a sense of control and autonomy over one's sensory experiences.

In the digital age, assistive tools and technology offer innovative solutions for sensory regulation, empowering individuals to tailor their environments to meet their unique sensory needs. Sensory apps, for example, can help manage sensory input by providing customizable soundscapes, visual stimuli, or guided relaxation exercises, all accessible at one's fingertips. Wearable technology, such as stress-monitoring wristbands, can alert individuals to stress-related physiological changes, allowing for proactive management of sensory overload. When integrated into daily life, these tools serve as allies in the quest for sensory balance, offering personalized support that enhances overall well-being. As we continue to explore the intersection of technology and sensory regulation, embracing these advancements as part of a holistic approach to managing sensory overload is crucial, recognizing the potential they hold to transform our interactions with the world around us.

1.10 Self-Care Practices: Prioritizing Your Mental Well-Being

In the bustling pace of modern life, self-care is often relegated to the periphery, perceived as a luxury rather than a necessity. Yet, for autistic individuals, self-care serves as a vital pillar of mental well-being, a lifeline that can significantly reduce stress and promote overall health. Consider self-care as replenishing one's internal reserves, akin to regularly charging a battery that powers your daily activities. Dedicating time to self-care, fortifies your mental resilience and enhances your capacity to engage with the world more balanced and harmoniously. This is not merely about indulging in occasional treats or moments of solitude; it is about committing to a consistent practice that nurtures your mental, emotional, and physical health holistically. Regular self-care acts as a buffer against the relentless demands of life, allowing you to navigate challenges with more remarkable poise and equanimity.

Creating a personalized self-care routine is an endeavor that requires introspection and intentionality. Begin by identifying activities that bring you joy and relaxation, those moments that allow you to disconnect from external pressures and reconnect with your inner self. This might include scheduling daily relaxation activities such as reading a favorite book, listening to calming music, or practicing deep breathing exercises. Incorporate hobbies and interests into your routine, as these pursuits provide a sense of fulfillment and purpose, counterbalancing daily life's rigors. Remember that your self-care routine should be as unique as you are, tailored to fit your individual needs and preferences. The key lies in consistency, ensuring that self-care becomes an integral part of your daily rhythm rather than a sporadic indulgence.

Physical activity is a potent component of self-care, offering many benefits beyond the physical realm. Doing gentle exercises such as yoga or tai chi can enhance flexibility and strength while promoting relaxation and mindfulness. These practices encourage a connection between body and mind, fostering an awareness of breath and movement that can alleviate stress and anxiety. Whether a leisurely walk in the park or a more vigorous hike, outdoor activities provide an opportunity to immerse oneself in nature, reaping the mood-enhancing effects of fresh air and natural surroundings. Physical activity invigorates the body and the spirit, offering a sense of vitality and well-being that permeates all aspects of life.

Balancing self-care with daily responsibilities is a delicate dance that necessitates setting realistic goals and integrating self-care into your routines. Approach self-care goals flexibly, acknowledging that some days may afford more time and energy than others. Rather than viewing self-care as an isolated task, consider how it can be woven into your daily activities. This might involve taking mindful breaks during work, savoring moments of stillness amidst a busy schedule, or practicing gratitude as part of your morning routine. By embedding self-care into the fabric of your day-to-day life, you create a sustainable practice that nurtures your well-being without detracting from your responsibilities. It is about finding harmony between caring for yourself and fulfilling the demands of life, ensuring that you are equipped to meet each day with renewed strength and clarity.

1.11 Accessing Mental Health Resources: Finding the Right Support

Navigating the landscape of mental health can feel like traversing an intricate maze, especially when trying to discern and articulate your own mental health needs. It requires a deep self-awareness and honesty, acknowledging when self-help strategies—though invaluable—may not suffice. Imagine standing at a crossroads, where the familiar paths of self-reliance meet the unknown avenues of professional assistance. Here, recognizing the signs indicating the need for professional support becomes crucial. These signs may manifest as persistent feelings of distress, overwhelming anxiety, or a pervasive sense of being stuck despite your best efforts. Acknowledging these signals is not indicative of failure but a testament to your courage in seeking a more profound understanding and support.

The quest for suitable mental health professionals, particularly those who understand the nuanced needs of autistic individuals, requires both diligence and discernment. Autism-friendly therapists with clinical acumen, empathy, and understanding of neurodiverse experiences are indispensable allies in this journey. They provide a safe space to explore your thoughts and emotions without fear of judgment. When searching for such professionals, consider contacting local autism networks or utilizing online directories that specialize in connecting neurodivergent individuals with appropriate therapists. The advent of teletherapy has further expanded access to mental health support, offering convenience and flexibility. This modality enables you to engage in therapy from the comfort of your own space, eliminating geographical constraints and allowing for a more personalized therapeutic experience.

Community support options are integral to mental health care, offering a sense of belonging and shared understanding. Participating in support groups for autistic individuals can provide a platform for connection, where shared experiences become a source of mutual support and encouragement. These in-person or online groups offer a space to share your challenges and triumphs with others who truly understand. Community wellness programs, often facilitated by local organizations, provide additional opportunities for engagement and support, promoting holistic well-being through workshops, activities, and educational resources. These community-based initiatives enhance mental health and foster a sense of community and camaraderie, reminding you that you are not alone in your experiences.

Navigating the complexities of mental health systems can be daunting, yet understanding these systems is crucial for accessing the support you need. Begin by familiarizing yourself with the intricacies of insurance coverage for mental health services, as this knowledge can help you make informed decisions about your care options. Contact insurance providers for detailed information on coverage specifics, including eligible services and potential out-of-pocket costs. Advocacy for necessary mental health accommodations is another vital aspect of navigating these systems. This involves confidently articulating your needs to healthcare providers and ensuring your unique requirements are met with empathy and understanding. Whether it's requesting specific accommodations during therapy sessions or seeking referrals to specialists, advocating for yourself within these systems is a decisive step toward ensuring that your mental health care is both comprehensive and tailored to your needs.

The underlying theme of this multifaceted exploration of mental health resources is empowerment. By actively engaging with these resources, you are taking charge of your mental health journey, equipping yourself with the knowledge and support needed to thrive. Remember that seeking help is a sign of strength, an acknowledgment that you are worthy of care and support in your quest for well-being.

1.12 Building Resilience: Thriving Amidst Challenges

Resilience is the quiet strength that allows individuals to rebound from adversity with vigor and determination. For autistic individuals, this concept takes on unique significance, as it involves navigating a world that can often feel unaccommodating and perplexing. Resilient individuals are characterized by their ability to adapt to change, maintain focus under pressure, and approach life's challenges with optimism and hope. They possess an unwavering belief in their capacity to overcome obstacles, viewing setbacks not as insurmountable barriers but as opportunities for growth and learning. The impact of resilience on mental health is profound, offering a buffer against the deleterious effects of stress and anxiety and fostering a sense of agency and empowerment. By cultivating resilience, autistic individuals can enhance their ability to manage life's vicissitudes, ensuring a more balanced and fulfilling existence.

Developing resilience involves a deliberate and mindful approach to life's challenges, transforming past experiences into stepping stones for future strength. Reflecting on past adversities and extracting the lessons they imparted is instrumental in building resilience. This reflective practice allows individuals to recognize patterns of behavior and response that have served them well and identify areas for improvement. Through this introspection, one can develop robust problem-solving skills, honing the ability to approach challenges with creativity and resourcefulness. By viewing problems as puzzles to be solved rather than insurmountable hurdles, individuals can foster a sense of competence and confidence in their ability to navigate life's complexities. This shift in perspective enhances resilience and encourages a proactive approach to life's challenges, empowering individuals to take control of their circumstances.

Cultivating a positive mindset is a cornerstone of resilience, which involves nurturing gratitude and optimism in the face of adversity. Practicing gratitude, whether through journaling or daily reflection, invites individuals to focus on the positive aspects of their lives, fostering a sense of contentment and appreciation. Positive affirmations, simple yet powerful statements reinforcing one's strengths and abilities, can be daily reminders of one's worth and potential. Reframing challenges as opportunities for growth rather than threats to be feared encourages a mindset that embraces change and uncertainty with openness and curiosity. This reframing process transforms adversity into a catalyst for personal development, inviting individuals to explore new possibilities and perspectives. By adopting a positive mindset, individuals can enhance their resilience, equipping themselves with the mental fortitude needed to thrive amidst life's challenges.

Creating a supportive environment is integral to fostering resilience, as it provides the foundation upon which individuals can build their strength and adaptability. Building strong social connections, whether through family, friends, or community groups, offers a network of support that can be relied upon in times of need. These connections provide harmony and emotional support, offering encouragement and understanding when challenges arise. Encouraging open communication and support within these networks and fostering trust and mutual respect are vital. Individuals can enhance their resilience by cultivating an environment that values collaboration and empathy, knowing they are supported by a community that understands and values their unique strengths. This supportive environment bolsters individual resilience and contributes to a collective sense of empowerment and solidarity, creating a community that thrives together.

In the tapestry of resilience, each thread represents an opportunity for growth and transformation. By nurturing resilience, individuals enhance their well-being and contribute to a broader culture of empowerment and understanding. As you continue to explore and cultivate resilience, remember that this is a dynamic and ongoing process that requires patience and perseverance. Embrace life's challenges and opportunities, knowing you possess the strength and resilience to navigate them with gracefully and confidently. The journey toward resilience is one of discovery and empowerment, a testament to the indomitable spirit that resides within each of us.

Book 2: The Book of Social Skills and Relationships

Imagine standing at the side of a grand ballroom, the air humming with lively discussion and giggling, yet seeming like an unnoticeable obstacle between you and the remainder of the world. For several autistic people, social communication can usually feel in this manner--mystical and also elusive, like dancing where everybody else appears to understand the actions. The complexities of social involvement are not merely regarding trading words; instead, they include a harmony of spoken and non-verbal hints, each adding to the tune of the link. As we check out the structures of reliable interaction, it's essential to acknowledge that interaction is intensely individual, differing commonly throughout the autistic neighborhood.

Whether via comprehensive spoken exchanges or the nuanced language of motions and expressions, comprehending your interaction design is vital to browsing social landscapes with self-confidence and credibility.

Within the abundant tapestry of interaction designs, autistic people frequently display a variety that mirrors their one-of-a-kind points of view and experiences.

Some might discover convenience in a spoken expression, where language is a device for enthusiastically sharing detailed ideas. In contrast, others might inclined to non-verbal interaction, where motions, facial expressions, and silence hold extensive significance. It is necessary to recognize individual interaction toughness, acknowledging that there is no particular "correct" means to connect.

You could locate solace in the accuracy of created words where ideas can be meticulously considered and expressed. Or perhaps your interaction thrives in the world of non-verbal signals where a glimpse or a motion imparts quantities greater than talked language ever before could. By welcoming your private design, you lay the foundation for authentic and efficient communication that values and commemorates the variety of interactions within the autistic neighborhood.

2.1 Interactive Element: Reflective Listening Exercise

Active listening represents a cornerstone of effective communication, a skill that transcends the mere act of hearing words and delves into the art of truly understanding another's perspective. It involves listening to the content of what is being said and attending to the emotions and intentions behind the words. Reflective listening, a technique in which you paraphrase or summarize what the other person has said, is a powerful tool in this endeavor. Doing so demonstrates empathy and understanding, creating a space where the speaker feels valued and heard. Maintaining eye contact, though often challenging for autistic individuals, can enhance this connection, signaling engagement and attentiveness. Yet, it is essential to approach eye contact flexibly, recognizing that comfort levels vary and that the absence of eye contact does not equate to disinterest. Instead, consider other ways to convey attentiveness, such as nodding or providing verbal affirmations, ensuring that your listening is active and supportive.

Expressing thoughts clearly can sometimes feel like navigating a labyrinth, where the path to clarity is obscured by the complexities of language and interpretation. Strategies for articulation begin with using concise language, distilling thoughts into their essence without sacrificing depth or nuance. Visual aids, such as diagrams or written summaries, can further enhance communication, providing a tangible anchor for abstract ideas. Structuring conversations with clear points and transitions helps maintain focus and coherence, guiding the listener through the narrative quickly. Through these techniques, you can convey your thoughts with precision and impact, ensuring your audience understands your message.

Communication barriers, those invisible yet formidable obstacles, often arise from sensory overload, misunderstandings, or differing interpretations of language. For autistic individuals, managing sensory overload during conversations is crucial, as overwhelming stimuli can hinder effective communication. Techniques such as deep breathing, taking breaks, or finding quieter environments can mitigate these challenges, allowing for more focused and meaningful interactions. Technology offers innovative solutions, with communication apps and devices facilitating expression and understanding. From text-to-speech software to visual communication boards, these tools empower individuals to communicate in ways that align with their preferences and needs, bridging gaps and fostering connection.

Try this exercise to enhance your active listening skills. Partner with a friend or family member and share a brief story or experience. As the listener, focus on paraphrasing or summarizing the speaker has shared, ensuring that your response captures the essence of their message. Switch roles and repeat the exercise, reflecting on how it feels to be both the speaker and the listener. Consider how reflective listening deepens your understanding and connection, and incorporate this practice into your daily interactions.

As we explore the intricacies of communication, remember that it is not about adhering to a predetermined set of rules but rather about crafting a dialogue that honors your individuality and the shared humanity of those around you. By embracing the diverse tapestry of communication styles, you empower yourself and others to engage in genuine, meaningful, and transformative conversations.

2.2 Understanding Social Cues: Practical Techniques for Connection

Navigating the complex landscape of social interactions requires more than just understanding verbal communication; it necessitates a keen awareness of the subtleties of body language and non-verbal signals, which often convey as much meaning as spoken words. Decoding body language can feel like learning a new dialect, one where the nuances of a raised eyebrow or the angle of a shoulder carry significant weight. Facial expressions, for instance, are a rich tapestry of emotion, with a slight upturn of the lips suggesting amusement and furrowed brows indicating concern. Each gesture, whether a nod of affirmation or crossed arms suggesting defensiveness, provides insight into the thoughts and emotions of those around us. Understanding posture, such as leaning forward in engagement or reclining in disinterest, offers additional layers of meaning in these non-verbal communications. For those on the spectrum, reading these cues can transform our interactions, allowing us to engage more deeply and authentically with others.

Beyond the physicality of gestures and expressions lies the intricate interplay of tone and context, both pivotal in discerning the true intention behind words. Tone, with its myriad variations, can change the nature of a message entirely—sarcasm, for example, often employs a contradictory tone to the words spoken, requiring the listener to discern the intended meaning. Sincerity, conversely, is frequently marked by a gentle, earnest tone. The context in which a conversation occurs adds another dimension, providing clues that help decode the message. A joke shared among close friends may be interpreted differently in a formal setting, where the context dictates a more reserved approach. These subtle nuances are critical in navigating social interactions, allowing us to respond appropriately and maintain the flow of conversation. Recognizing and understanding these elements can be challenging, yet they are invaluable tools in our social toolkit.

Responding to social cues with precision is an art form that involves aligning our verbal responses with the non-verbal signals we perceive. Imagine a conductor synchronizing the various sections of an orchestra to create a harmonious symphony; similarly, our responses must be attuned to the cues around us to ensure a seamless interaction. Matching verbal responses to non-verbal cues might mean offering a comforting word to someone whose body language suggests distress or sharing in laughter when a smile lights up a room. Practicing situational role-plays with supportive friends or mentors can provide a safe space to explore and refine these skills, offering immediate feedback and fostering confidence in real-world applications. Such exercises help us develop a repertoire of genuine and contextually appropriate responses, enhancing our ability to connect with others meaningfully.

Engage in interactive games to enhance your recognition and response to social cues. Gather a group of friends or peers and participate in activities where you identify and interpret non-verbal signals. Each participant can take turns acting out various emotions or scenarios using only body language and facial expressions while the others attempt to interpret the cues. This exercise sharpens your ability to read social cues. It offers an opportunity for peer feedback, fostering a collaborative learning environment where you can gain insights into how your interpretations align with others'.

As we immerse ourselves in social cues, we must approach these interactions with curiosity and openness, recognizing that mastery comes through practice and patience. The ability to read and respond to social cues is not confined to a single formula but is an evolving skill that grows with experience and reflection. By engaging with these techniques and exercises, you empower yourself to navigate social landscapes confidently and clearly, forging authentic and rewarding connections.

2.3 Strengthening Personal Relationships: Empathy and Understanding

Empathy is the connective tissue of human relationships, the invisible thread that binds us to one another through mutual understanding and shared experience. For autistic individuals, cultivating empathy can feel like learning to tune into a frequency that is often drowned out by the cacophony of societal expectations and misunderstandings. Yet, empathy is not an innate trait exclusive to a select few; it is a skill that can be nurtured and developed through deliberate practice and perspective-taking. Perspective-taking, the ability to step into another's shoes and view the world from their vantage point, is a powerful exercise in empathy-building. It requires an openness to the kaleidoscope of human experience, inviting us to consider the emotions and motivations that drive others' actions. Empathy-building exercises, such as reflecting on shared experiences or engaging in active listening, can further enhance our capacity for empathy, fostering deeper connections with those around us. By embracing the practice of empathy, we cultivate relationships that are not only robust but also profound in their understanding and acceptance of our shared humanity.

Building trust and rapport within relationships lays the foundation for meaningful and enduring connections, yet it is a process that demands both time and consistency. Trust is not granted; it is earned through actions that demonstrate reliability and integrity. The consistency with which we show up in our interactions, whether through small gestures or significant commitments, signals to others that we are dependable and trustworthy. This consistency is complemented by establishing and respecting boundaries that delineate the space within which trust can flourish. Boundaries are not barriers but markers of mutual respect and understanding, ensuring that each individual's needs and limits are acknowledged and honored. Setting boundaries involves open communication and negotiation, creating a framework for trust to thrive. Maintaining this framework fosters an environment of safety and security, allowing relationships to deepen and evolve.

Effective communication within relationships is akin to a well-choreographed dance, where each partner moves harmoniously, guided by open and honest dialogue. Such communication is the lifeblood of any relationship, facilitating the expression of needs, desires, and emotions in an authentic and considerate manner. Active listening, a cornerstone of effective communication, involves hearing the words spoken and attuning to the feelings and intentions underpinning them. It is a practice that requires patience and presence, allowing us to fully engage with our loved ones and respond with empathy and understanding. Communicating needs and desires clearly, without ambiguity or assumption, further strengthens this dialogue, ensuring that both parties feel heard and valued. By embracing these communication tools, we create a dynamic of mutual respect and support, enriching our relationships with depth and authenticity.

Maintaining healthy relationships over time requires a commitment to ongoing care and attention, much like tending to a garden that flourishes through regular nurturing. Regularly scheduled check-ins, whether over coffee or phone calls from afar, serve as touchpoints for connection and reflection, allowing us to address any concerns or celebrate shared successes. These check-ins provide an opportunity to navigate changes and challenges together, reinforcing the shared commitment to the relationship's growth and vitality. Life is inherently dynamic, and relationships must adapt to the evolving circumstances and milestones that arise. By approaching these changes with flexibility and openness, we foster resilience within our relationships, ensuring they remain strong and supportive amidst the shifting tides of life.

Empathy and understanding act as guiding lights in the intricate dance of relationships, illuminating the path toward more profound connection and mutual respect. Through the cultivation of compassion, the building of trust, the practice of effective communication, and the maintenance of healthy dynamics, we create relationships that are not only enduring but also enriching. These relationships, grounded in authenticity and acceptance, serve as sanctuaries of support and encouragement, nurturing our growth and well-being as we navigate the complexities of life. As we continue to engage with these practices, we empower ourselves to forge meaningful and transformative connections, contributing to a tapestry of relationships that celebrate the diversity and richness of the human experience.

2.4 Navigating Social Anxiety: Strategies for Comfort and Ease

The feeling of social anxiety, particularly within the context of autism, can be as pervasive as it is debilitating, often casting a shadow over interactions that others might find routine. It manifests as an acute awareness of social settings and an overwhelming fear of negative evaluation or judgment. For autistic individuals, social anxiety may be further exacerbated by the sensory sensitivities and communication challenges that are inherent to the condition. The distinction between situational and chronic anxiety is crucial here. Situational anxiety typically arises in specific contexts, such as public speaking or meeting new people.

In contrast, chronic anxiety is more persistent, lingering beneath the surface and affecting a broader range of interactions. Identifying the triggers of this anxiety, whether they be crowded environments, unstructured social events, or the unpredictability of conversation, is a vital step in mitigating its impact. By understanding these triggers, one can develop strategies that provide comfort and ease in navigating social landscapes.

Practical coping mechanisms are indispensable tools in managing social anxiety, offering a means to reclaim a sense of control and tranquility amidst the turmoil. Deep breathing exercises anchor in moments of heightened anxiety, promoting relaxation by slowing the heart rate and calming the mind. Grounding techniques, which involve focusing on the present moment through sensory experiences, can also be incredibly effective. For example, naming objects in a room or feeling the texture of an item can draw attention away from anxious thoughts and back to a state of calm. Creating a social script for common scenarios, such as introductions or small talk, provides a structured framework for interaction, reducing uncertainty and fostering confidence. These scripts act as a roadmap, guiding you through the intricacies of conversation with clarity and assurance. By rehearsing these scripts in advance, you can approach social situations with a sense of preparedness and poise, transforming anxiety into a manageable component of your social repertoire.

The concept of gradual exposure is foundational in treating social anxiety, embodying the principle of desensitization through incremental challenges. By slowly increasing social exposure, individuals can acclimate to the stimuli that typically trigger anxiety, reducing their impact over time. It is akin to dipping one's toes into a pool before wading in, allowing for acclimatization at a comfortable pace. Starting with small, non-threatening gatherings, such as a coffee date with a close friend, provides a gentle introduction to social interaction. As comfort and confidence grow, the complexity of social settings can be gradually increased, progressing to larger gatherings or more dynamic environments. This methodical approach not only builds resilience but also empowers individuals to expand their social horizons without the overwhelming fear of drowning in anxiety. Through each successive exposure, the perceived threat diminishes, replaced by a newfound sense of capability and assurance.

Building social confidence is an ongoing endeavor involving both introspection and practice. Positive visualization exercises can be powerful, inviting you to imagine yourself succeeding in social situations with confidence and ease. By visualizing favorable outcomes and rehearsing your responses in your mind, you lay the groundwork for real-world success. Role-playing social interactions with a trusted friend or mentor can further enhance this confidence, providing a supportive environment to experiment with different approaches and receive constructive feedback. These role-plays mimic real-life scenarios, offering a safe space to explore and refine social skills. With each practice session, confidence grows, paving the way for more authentic and engaging interactions.

The journey through social anxiety is not a solitary endeavor; it is enriched by the support and understanding of those around you. By embracing strategies that promote comfort and ease, you empower yourself to engage in social interactions with greater assurance, transforming anxiety from a barrier into a bridge that connects you to the world.

2.5 Finding Your Tribe: Building Supportive Communities

Finding one's tribe is profoundly personal and transformative, touching the core of identity and belonging. For autistic individuals, discovering a community that resonates with personal experiences and aspirations can be challenging and rewarding. To embark on this search, identify what you seek in a supportive community. Consider aligning with groups that reflect your interests and values, from shared hobbies and professional pursuits to advocacy and neurodiversity appreciation. Assessing the level of engagement and interaction you desire is crucial—some may find solace in small, intimate gatherings, while others may thrive in dynamic, more prominent groups. By clearly defining these parameters, you can ensure that the communities you engage with enrich your life and provide the understanding and empathy you seek.

Exploring existing communities aligning with these criteria is the next step, and myriad avenues exist. Local autism support groups often serve as a haven for connection and mutual support, offering a space where shared experiences foster a sense of belonging. These groups can be found through community centers, local advocacy organizations, or mental health professionals who may have resources or recommendations. In addition to in-person gatherings, online forums for neurodiversity provide an expansive platform for connection, transcending geographical limitations and bringing together individuals from diverse backgrounds. These digital spaces, whether through social media groups, dedicated forums, or virtual meet-ups, offer a unique opportunity to engage with a global community, sharing insights, advice, and solidarity. By actively participating in these communities, you expand your network and contribute to a collective tapestry of support and empowerment.

Should existing communities fall short of your needs, building new communities can be exciting and daunting. Yet, the rewards of creating a space that truly reflects your values and interests are immeasurable. Starting a local meet-up group can be rewarding to bring together like-minded individuals in your area. Begin by identifying a common interest or goal and reaching out to potential members through local bulletin boards, social media, or community events. Organize initial gatherings in accessible and welcoming locations, fostering an environment that encourages open dialogue and connection. Alternatively, creating an online group or forum can be a valuable resource for those seeking a broader reach. Platforms such as Facebook or Reddit offer tools for establishing groups where you can set the tone and purpose for interactions, ensuring that the community remains inclusive and supportive.

Maintaining community engagement is essential to the longevity and vibrancy of any group, requiring ongoing effort and creativity. Regular events and activities keep members connected and invested, providing opportunities for interaction and collaboration. These events range from informal coffee chats and workshops to larger gatherings or guest speaker sessions. Consider incorporating a variety of formats to cater to different preferences and encourage diverse participation. Implementing feedback systems is equally important, allowing members to share their thoughts and suggestions for improvement. This might involve surveys, suggestion boxes, or open forums where members can voice their opinions. By valuing and incorporating feedback, you demonstrate a commitment to the community's growth and adaptation, ensuring that it continues to meet the evolving needs of its members.

In finding your tribe, you embark on a journey of discovery and connection, where the relationships you forge become a source of strength and inspiration. Whether through existing groups or new communities you create, the bonds you build offer a sanctuary of understanding and support, enriching your life in profound and meaningful ways. As you explore these connections, remember that the essence of a community lies in its diversity and inclusivity, celebrating the myriad voices and experiences that come together to form a cohesive whole. The path to finding your tribe is not linear, but it is a path filled with potential and promise, where each step taken brings you closer to a sense of belonging and purpose.

2.6 Online and Offline Networking: Creating Meaningful Connections

In the expansive tapestry of personal and professional growth, networking emerges as a vital thread that weaves together opportunities, resources, and relationships. Online and offline networking opens many possibilities, offering access to information, mentorship, and collaboration that can significantly propel your journey forward. It is not merely about exchanging business cards or collecting connections but about building meaningful relationships that provide mutual support and encouragement. Engaging with a diverse network allows you to draw from a wellspring of experiences and insights, fostering an environment where ideas can flourish and opportunities can be explored. Whether seeking career advancement, personal growth, or community involvement, a well-cultivated network is a cornerstone for achieving your aspirations.

Online platforms have revolutionized how we connect, offering a vast digital landscape where networks can be expanded with a button. Social media groups tailored to specific interests or professions serve as vibrant communities where like-minded individuals can engage in dialogue, share resources, and offer support. These platforms transcend geographical boundaries, allowing you to connect with individuals from diverse cultural and professional backgrounds. Participating in virtual conferences and webinars further amplifies this reach, providing access to expert insights and discussions that can enrich your understanding and expand your network. By actively engaging in these online spaces, you increase your visibility and position yourself as a valuable contributor, fostering relationships leading to collaborative ventures and shared success.

While the digital realm offers unparalleled connectivity, the value of face-to-face interactions in building strong relationships remains irreplaceable. There's a unique authenticity and depth to in-person connections that digital interactions often struggle to replicate. Attending local events and workshops related to your interests or professional field offers an opportunity to engage directly with others, facilitating spontaneous and genuine interactions that can form the basis of enduring relationships. Volunteer opportunities in autism advocacy or other community initiatives provide a platform to work alongside others towards a common goal, strengthening bonds through shared purpose. These face-to-face interactions allow for the nuances of body language and tone to complement verbal communication, creating a more holistic and enriching experience that can deepen relational ties.

Balancing the digital and physical worlds of networking requires intentionality and strategy, ensuring that each realm complements and enhances the other. Setting clear goals for your networking activities can guide your efforts, whether expanding professional connections, seeking mentorship, or engaging with community initiatives. These goals provide a framework for measuring progress and ensuring your networking endeavors align with your broader personal and professional objectives. Utilizing online connections to facilitate offline meet-ups is a powerful strategy for integrating these two worlds. For example, reaching out to an online contact to arrange a coffee meeting or attending a local event recommended by a digital group can bridge the gap between virtual and real-world interactions. This approach solidifies relationships and enriches your network with diverse perspectives and experiences.

When approached with authenticity and openness, networking is a conduit for growth and connection. It is not merely about expanding your contacts list but about cultivating meaningful, reciprocal, and enriching relationships. As you navigate the intricacies of online and offline networking, remember that each interaction holds the potential to transform your path, offering insights and opportunities that can profoundly shape your journey. By embracing the dynamic interplay of digital and in-person connections, you create a diverse and robust network that is a testament to the power of collaboration and community.

It is All About Community and Creating Meaningful Connections

When I began writing The Autism Guide for Adults, I wanted to create something to help people understand themselves better. Whether you were just diagnosed as an adult or have been navigating life with autism for years, this guide was meant to feel like a friend—someone who gets it.

Writing this book was a journey. It made me reflect on my own life—on all the confusing moments that didn't make sense until, one day, they finally did. When you're trying to assemble a puzzle, you suddenly find one piece that makes the whole thing more evident. That's what learning about my autism felt like. And that's what I hope this book can be for you—a piece that helps you see your whole picture more clearly.

Now, I need your help. If this book made a difference for you—maybe it gave you new insight, made you feel less alone, or just made you say, "Oh, wow, that's me!"—I would love it if you could share your thoughts in a review. It doesn't have to be long or fancy.

To make a difference, simply scan the QR code below (or link if you are reading by Kindle) and leave a review:

https://www.amazon.com/review/review-your-purchases/?asin=B0DSCMDVT2

Why does your review matter?

When people search for books on autism, reviews help them decide what's worth their time. Your words could encourage someone else to pick up this guide and find the understanding they've been looking for.

So, if The Autism Guide for Adults has helped you in any way, please consider leaving a review. You could inspire someone else to start their journey of self-discovery, and if you love helping others, you're the person I am.

Thank you for being part of this. It is all about Community and creating Meaningful Connections, and your voice matters!

With gratitude,
JJ Andrade

2.7 Managing Complex Relationships: Boundaries and Expectations

Boundaries are often regarded as the bedrock of healthy relationships, providing the structural integrity necessary for mutual respect and understanding. Boundaries are the invisible lines delineating where one person ends and another begins, encompassing physical, emotional, and digital realms. Physical boundaries refer to personal space and touch, emotional boundaries involve the management of feelings and emotional responsibilities, and digital boundaries pertain to technology and online interactions. Recognizing and respecting these boundaries is crucial, as they protect individual autonomy and foster an environment where both parties can thrive. Personal boundary needs are unique and shaped by individual preferences, past experiences, and values. To navigate relationships effectively, reflecting on and communicating these needs is essential to ensure that both partners are on the same page.

Setting and communicating boundaries is a nuanced skill that requires clarity and assertiveness, yet it is an invaluable tool for building and maintaining healthy relationships. Articulating boundaries involves firmly and respectfully limits and expressing personal needs. Phrases such as "I need some time to process my thoughts before discussing this further" or "I'm comfortable sharing this much, but I'd like to keep other aspects private" can serve as templates for boundary setting. Practicing boundary conversations in safe and supportive environments can bolster confidence, allowing language and delivery to be refined before addressing more challenging situations. It's important to remember that setting boundaries is not about creating barriers but fostering a space where each individual feels safe, respected, and valued.

Managing expectations within relationships is another critical component that ensures mutual understanding and satisfaction. Expectations can often be the source of conflict if not clearly communicated and aligned between parties. It's beneficial to clarify expectations from the outset and discuss shared goals, responsibilities, and desires to prevent misunderstandings. This initial alignment creates a foundation upon which the relationship can build, minimizing the potential for disappointment or resentment. However, relationships are dynamic, and expectations may evolve, necessitating regular revisitation and adjustment. Scheduling periodic check-ins to revisit and discuss expectations allows for flexibility and adaptation, ensuring that both partners remain attuned to each other's needs and priorities.

Navigating relationship challenges is an inevitable aspect of maintaining complex relationships, yet it is also an opportunity for growth and strengthening bonds. Conflict resolution techniques, such as active listening, empathy, and compromise, are invaluable in addressing and resolving disagreements. Open dialogue, where both parties feel heard and understood, is essential to finding mutually acceptable solutions. In some cases, seeking mediation or third-party support, such as a therapist or counselor, can provide an objective perspective and facilitate productive conversations. These professionals can offer tools and strategies for managing conflict, ensuring that challenges are addressed constructively rather than destructively.

Building and sustaining friendships is akin to cultivating a garden, requiring ongoing care, attention, and nourishment. Friendships thrive on shared experiences, mutual support, and the willingness to invest time and effort into maintaining the connection. Regular communication keeps the relationship alive and vibrant, whether through scheduled meet-ups, phone calls, or messages. Additionally, navigating changes and challenges together, such as life transitions or personal difficulties, can strengthen the bond, reinforcing the trust and understanding that underpin the friendship. You create a nurturing environment where both parties can flourish by approaching friendships with intention and openness.

Romantic relationships, with their unique dynamics and intricacies, present both opportunities and challenges. Understanding your partner's perspective and fostering empathy and appreciation for their experiences and emotions are paramount. This understanding is fundamental when navigating love on the spectrum, where communication styles, sensory sensitivities, and social preferences may differ. Open and honest dialogue about these differences can enhance intimacy and connection, allowing both partners to feel valued and accepted. Family dynamics also play a significant role in romantic relationships, influencing perceptions, expectations, and interactions. Fostering understanding and support within the family context can bolster the relationship, providing a network of encouragement and acceptance.

Online socialization, as a digital extension of interpersonal interactions, offers a unique platform for connection and engagement. Digital connections allow individuals to transcend geographical boundaries, providing access to diverse communities and perspectives. However, they also require the establishment of digital boundaries to protect privacy and well-being. Balancing online interactions with offline connections is key to maintaining a healthy social life, ensuring that the digital realm enhances rather than replaces face-to-face relationships.

Parenting as a neurodivergent individual presents challenges and joys, requiring a delicate balance of personal growth and familial responsibilities. Understanding and embracing your unique parenting style can foster a nurturing and supportive environment for you and your children. Seeking support from like-minded parents or parenting groups can offer valuable insights and encouragement, helping to navigate the complexities of parenting with confidence and resilience.

Often perceived as trivial, small talk is a social lubricant that facilitates deeper connections and relationships. For neurodivergent individuals, making small talk work involves finding topics of mutual interest and employing conversational techniques that feel authentic and comfortable. Practicing these interactions in low-pressure environments can enhance confidence, providing a foundation for more meaningful exchanges.

Understanding relationship dynamics is a multifaceted endeavor, one that requires empathy, communication, and adaptability. By embracing these principles, you empower yourself to navigate the complexities of relationships with grace and authenticity, fostering enriching and enduring connections.

2.8 Conflict Resolution: Turning Challenges into Opportunities

The nature of conflict is as multifaceted as the individuals who encounter it, often arising from misunderstandings, unmet expectations, or differing values. In interpersonal relationships, conflicts are not merely obstacles to be overcome but opportunities for growth and understanding. Identifying common causes of conflict requires introspection and honesty and asking critical questions about the needs and desires at play. Consider how miscommunication might have sown seeds of discord or how assumptions about others' intentions could have led to friction. By viewing conflict as an opportunity to learn and evolve, you open yourself to a transformative process. This shift in perspective allows for a more constructive approach, where conflicts become catalysts for deeper connection and insight rather than merely points of contention.

Effective conflict resolution strategies are essential for navigating these challenges with grace and empathy. Central to this process is active listening, a practice that involves fully engaging with the speaker and acknowledging their perspective. It is setting aside preconceived notions and hearing what the other person expresses verbally and non-verbally. Employing "I" statements to express feelings can further enhance this dialogue, shifting the focus from blame to personal experience. For example, saying, "I feel overlooked when decisions are made without my input," invites a more open and empathetic response than "You always ignore my opinions." This approach fosters a collaborative atmosphere where both parties feel heard and validated, paving the way for resolution.

In group settings, mediating conflicts requires a delicate balance of facilitation and guidance, ensuring that all voices are respected and considered. Open dialogue and discussion are crucial, creating a safe space where participants can express their thoughts and feelings without fear of judgment or retaliation. As a mediator, you encourage constructive conversation, guiding the group toward mutual understanding and agreement. Employing techniques such as setting ground rules for communication or designating speaking times can help manage the flow of discussion, ensuring that everyone has the opportunity to contribute. By fostering an inclusive environment, you empower the group to resolve conflicts collectively, drawing on its members' diverse perspectives and insights.

Reflecting on conflicts and extracting valuable lessons is a process that enriches personal growth and enhances future interactions. Journaling about conflict experiences allows you to explore and analyze the dynamics at play, uncovering patterns or triggers that may have contributed to the situation. This reflective practice provides clarity and invites introspection, offering insights into how similar conflicts might be handled differently in the future. Developing action plans for future conflicts is another valuable step, equipping you with strategies and tools to employ when tensions arise. Consider what approaches have been practical in the past or what new techniques might be explored. By proactively preparing for potential conflicts, you transform uncertainty into confidence, enhancing your ability to navigate interpersonal challenges with resilience and insight.

In the grand tapestry of life, conflicts are the threads that, when skillfully woven, add depth and complexity to our relationships. Conflicts become growth opportunities through understanding, empathy, and reflection, bringing us closer to the authentic connections we seek. As we explore this intricate dance of human interaction, remember that each step taken toward resolution is a testament to your commitment to personal and relational growth, paving the way for a future prosperous with understanding and possibility.

The intricacies of conflict resolution serve as a bridge to the next chapter, where the focus shifts to professional growth and career success. Understanding and resolving conflicts is relevant in personal spheres and pivotal in the workplace, where collaboration and communication are key. The following book will explore strategies for confidently navigating the professional realm and building on effective communication and relationship management foundations.

Book 3: The Book of Professional Growth and Career Success

Imagine basing on the precipice of your occupation, the immense landscape of expert chances spread out before you, each course standing for various possible futures. For several, this sight is thrilling, yet for others, it can be discouraging, a puzzle of options and opportunities that need mindful navigating. As an autistic adult or neurodivergent person, you might discover that the conventional job courses, as well as assumptions, do not fit you completely. This understanding, nevertheless, is not a restriction but an invitation to reassess what success indicates for you directly.

By recognizing your peculiar strengths and developing your best abilities and state of mind, you can shape a career that is not just about doing things but also straightening with your authentic self.

Determining the core abilities needed for your wanted job course approaches constructing a toolkit customized for the trip in advance. Start by mapping out the technological skills required by your picked market, which frequently develops the structure upon which you build your specialist skills.

Whether you're understanding coding languages for work in software program growth or developing logical abilities for a profession in information scientific research, these technological proficiencies are essential to your success.

Nonetheless, just as vital are soft skills-- those abstract top qualities that promote partnership and flexibility in the office. Abilities such as efficient interaction, team effort, and psychological knowledge not only improve your capacity to function in harmony with others but also equip you to browse the complexities of interpersonal characteristics with convenience. By growing these soft skills, you can place yourself on your own as an all-around and beneficial staff member geared up to prosper in varied specialist settings.

Cultivating a growth mindset is a transformative venture that drives your knowledge and opens possibilities.

This mindset is rooted in the idea that capacities can be created through commitment and effort, propelling your professional development and unlocking your potential. Think of the difficulties you experience not as difficult challenges but as important lessons that improve your abilities and strengths.

Determination becomes your ally, permitting you to recuperate from difficulties with restored vitality and decision-making. Adopting a growth mindset transforms your job into a dynamic arena where you can try out, discover, and succeed.

3.1 Interactive Element: Reflection and Goal Setting

Time management, the art of orchestrating your hours precisely and purposefully, is a critical skill in maximizing productivity and achieving career goals. Employ prioritization frameworks such as the Eisenhower Box, which helps distinguish between urgent and important tasks, ensuring that your efforts are aligned with your objectives. Tools like Trello or Asana offer digital platforms for tracking tasks and deadlines, providing a structured approach to managing your workload. By effectively managing your time, you create space for both professional responsibilities and personal reflection, striking a balance that supports holistic growth.

Setting professional goals provides a roadmap for your career, guiding your actions and aspirations with clarity and intention. The SMART goal-setting framework—specific, Measurable, Achievable, Relevant, and Time-bound—is a powerful tool for crafting inspiring and attainable goals. Regular self-assessment allows you to evaluate your progress, making adjustments to ensure your trajectory aligns with your evolving vision. These goals become the milestones that mark your journey, each achievement a testament to your perseverance and dedication.

Take a moment to reflect on your current skills and career objectives. Using the SMART framework, draft one short-term and one long-term professional goal. Consider what technical or soft skills you must develop to achieve these goals.

Regularly revisit and adjust your goals to align with your career growth and personal aspirations.

As you embark on this path of professional growth and career success, remember that your journey is uniquely yours, shaped by your strengths and aspirations. Embrace the opportunities for growth and learning, knowing that each step brings you closer to the career and life you envision.

3.2 Workplace Accommodations: Advocating for Your Needs

Navigating the workplace as an autistic individual requires an understanding of your rights and the laws designed to protect them. The Americans with Disabilities Act (ADA), a cornerstone of disability rights legislation in the United States, mandates that employers provide reasonable accommodations to qualified employees with disabilities, including autism. This legal framework ensures that you have the right to request modifications to your work environment that enable you to perform your job effectively. Similar laws exist globally, each tailored to their specific jurisdictions, offering a protective umbrella under which you can advocate for your needs. Familiarizing yourself with these laws is crucial, empowering you to confidently discuss accommodations with your employer. Many resources are available to help you understand workplace policies, such as guides from the Job Accommodation Network (JAN) or the Employer Assistance and Resource Network on

Disability Inclusion (EARN), which provide valuable insights and strategies for navigating these conversations.

Identifying the accommodations that will benefit you is a personalized process requiring introspection and awareness of your unique needs. Standard accommodations, such as flexible working hours, create a more conducive work environment. For instance, a later start time might assist in avoiding sensory overload during a hectic morning commute. Personalized workspace adjustments, such as noise-canceling headphones or a quiet area, can also play a pivotal role in enhancing focus and reducing stress. It is essential to consider your specific sensory preferences and executive functioning challenges when determining which accommodations will best support your productivity and well-being. By tailoring your environment to suit your needs, you create a workspace that fosters comfort and efficiency, allowing you to thrive in your role.

Effectively communicating your accommodation needs to your employer is a skill that, while challenging, can be honed with practice and preparation. Start by crafting a concise request that clearly outlines the accommodations you seek and the reasons they are necessary. It's helpful to frame your request in terms of how these modifications will enhance your performance and contribute to the overall success of the team or organization. Role-playing conversations with a trusted friend or mentor provide a safe space to practice articulating your needs, helping to build confidence and refine your approach. When meeting with your employer or HR representative, approach the conversation openly and collaboratively, emphasizing your commitment to contributing positively to the workplace while addressing your personal needs.

Building supportive relationships within the workplace is another key element of fostering an inclusive and accommodating environment. Finding allies and mentors among your colleagues can provide invaluable support and guidance, helping you navigate workplace dynamics more easily. These individuals can advocate for you, offer advice, and help create a culture of understanding and acceptance. Participating in employee resource groups dedicated to supporting neurodiverse employees can also provide a sense of community and belonging, allowing you to connect with others who share similar experiences and challenges. By cultivating these relationships, you enhance your work experience and contribute to a more inclusive workplace culture that values diversity and collaboration.

You pave the way for a fulfilling and successful career by understanding your rights, identifying necessary accommodations, communicating effectively, and building supportive workplace relationships. This journey toward workplace empowerment is about advocating for your needs and contributing to a broader movement toward inclusivity and understanding in the professional world.

3.3 Career Development Paths: Leveraging Your Unique Strengths

Understanding and leveraging your unique strengths is pivotal in navigating the professional landscape with confidence and clarity. Each individual possesses a constellation of talents and capabilities that, when identified and nurtured, can illuminate their path to career success. Engaging in a strengths assessment, such as the DISC Personality Test, can provide valuable insights into your inherent propensities, highlighting areas where you naturally excel. This awareness is affirming and strategic, allowing you to align your career pursuits with your strengths, maximizing satisfaction and productivity. Consider the real-life example of an individual whose meticulous attention to detail and affinity for numbers led them to a successful career in data analysis. This role capitalized on their natural abilities while providing a sense of purpose and fulfillment.

Exploring diverse career paths that resonate with your personal strengths opens a world of possibilities beyond traditional roles. In a rapidly evolving job market, alternative career options offer unique opportunities to apply your skills innovatively. Non-linear career trajectories—those that diverge from the conventional ladder of progression—can be especially rewarding, allowing flexibility and adaptability in pursuing varied interests and passions. This approach broadens your professional horizons and fosters a dynamic and fulfilling career journey where the path is as significant as the destination. By embracing the potential of diverse career paths, you empower yourself to pursue roles that are not only aligned with your strengths but also reflective of your evolving aspirations and values.

Networking with purpose is a powerful tool for building professional connections that support and advance your career aspirations. Rather than approaching networking as a transactional exercise, consider it an opportunity to cultivate meaningful relationships with individuals who share your interests and values. Attending industry-specific conferences can provide a fertile ground for such connections, offering access to thought leaders, potential mentors, and like-minded peers. Similarly, leveraging platforms like LinkedIn allows you to engage with a global network of professionals, facilitating connections that can lead to mentorship opportunities, collaborations, and career advancement. By approaching networking with intention and authenticity, you create a supportive community that propels you toward your professional goals while offering reciprocal support and inspiration.

Continuous skill enhancement is a cornerstone of sustained career growth, allowing you to remain agile and competitive in an ever-changing job market. Online courses and certifications through platforms like EdX provide flexible opportunities to deepen your expertise, acquire new skills, and stay abreast of industry developments. This commitment to lifelong learning enriches your professional capabilities and fosters a curiosity and innovation mindset. Seeking feedback and mentorship further enhances your growth, offering insights and guidance from those who have traversed similar paths. Engaging with mentors provides a valuable opportunity to learn from their experiences, gain perspective on your journey, and receive constructive feedback informing your development. By embracing continuous skill enhancement, you position yourself as a proactive and adaptive professional, ready to seize opportunities and confidently navigate challenges.

3.4 Job Search Strategies: Tailoring Your Approach for Success

The job search process often feels like an intricate dance, requiring precision and adaptability. Crafting a resume and cover letter that stand out is crucial to capturing the attention of potential employers. This involves more than just listing your skills and experiences; it's about customizing these documents to reflect the specific demands of each job application. Start by scrutinizing the job description and identifying keywords that highlight what the employer is seeking. Integrate these keywords seamlessly into your resume and cover letter, ensuring your relevant skills and experiences shine through. For instance, if an employer emphasizes teamwork and problem-solving, weave these terms into your descriptions, illustrating your proficiency with concrete examples. This aligns your application with the employer's needs and demonstrates your attention to detail and understanding of the role.

In the digital age, job search platforms are indispensable tools for discovering opportunities and making connections. LinkedIn, with its vast professional network, is a particularly valuable resource. Navigating its job search tools allows you to filter positions that match your skills and interests while providing insights into company culture and expectations. Engaging with recruitment agencies can also open doors to unadvertised opportunities, as these agencies often have direct lines to employers seeking specific talents. When working with recruiters, be clear about your career goals and preferences, enabling them to match you with fitting opportunities. Utilizing these platforms expands your reach and increases your chances of finding a role that aligns with your aspirations.

Personal and professional networks offer many opportunities during the job search process, often serving as conduits to positions that might not be publicly listed. Informational interviews with industry professionals provide a window into a company's or field's inner workings, offering insights that can inform your application and interview strategy. These informal conversations can also lead to referrals or introductions to other key contacts. Attending networking events and job fairs allows you to engage with employers face-to-face, presenting a chance to make a memorable impression. Though sometimes challenging, these interactions can be invaluable in building relationships and gaining visibility within your desired industry. Approach these events with curiosity and openness, viewing each encounter as a potential stepping stone toward your career objectives.

The rise of virtual job searches presents its own set of challenges and opportunities. In this digital landscape, creating a professional online presence is paramount. Ensure your LinkedIn profile is polished and up-to-date, reflecting your skills, experiences, and career aspirations. Consider sharing articles or insights about your field, showcasing your expertise, and engaging with industry trends. Virtual networking, whether through LinkedIn or industry-specific online communities, offers a comfortable platform for building connections without the sensory overload that in-person events can sometimes entail. Techniques for virtual networking include reaching out with personalized messages, engaging in meaningful conversations, and following up with individuals you connect with. These digital interactions can foster relationships leading to job opportunities and collaborations, proving that the virtual realm is just as fertile for professional growth as the physical one.

3.5 Mastering the Interview: Authenticity as Your Strength

Imagine the interview room as a stage where your unique story unfolds, a space where authenticity shines as your greatest asset. To prepare effectively, immerse yourself in understanding the company's culture and values, much like an explorer familiarizing themselves with a new terrain. This knowledge equips you to align your narratives with the company's ethos, illustrating your professional fit and genuine interest in their mission. As you practice responses to common interview questions, focus on crafting answers that integrate your personal experiences and insights. This isn't about rehearsing a script but finding the words that resonate with your truth. Familiarize yourself with the STAR method—Situation, Task, Action, Result—a framework that enables you to structure your responses with clarity and impact, transforming abstract qualities into tangible narratives.

Authenticity in communication is not merely a strategy but a reflection of who you are. As you share personal stories during the interview, allow your passion and enthusiasm to come through. These stories are the threads that weave together your experiences, highlighting how past challenges have shaped your strengths and aspirations. Rather than presenting a façade of perfection, embrace vulnerability; acknowledge learning moments and how they have contributed to your growth. This transparency humanizes you and establishes a rapport with the interviewer, inviting them to see you as a potential colleague who brings both skill and sincerity.

Handling interview challenges requires a blend of preparation and adaptability. Interview anxiety is an everyday companion, but it need not be an adversary. Techniques such as deep breathing or visualization can help center you, transforming nervous energy into focus. Addressing potential gaps in your employment history with honesty and context can turn perceived weaknesses into resilience reflections. Frame these periods as opportunities for personal development, emphasizing the skills acquired and the insights gained. This narrative reframing demonstrates your ability to adapt to life's ebbs and flows, reinforcing your resilience and readiness to contribute meaningfully to the company.

Post-interview follow-up is an art that extends beyond mere courtesy. Creating personalized thank-you emails is an opportunity to reiterate your enthusiasm and reflect on specific aspects of the conversation that resonated with you. This attention to detail reinforces your interest and keeps you in the interviewer's mind. As you reflect on the interview experience, consider what went well and what could be improved. This introspection is invaluable, offering insights that refine your approach for future opportunities. Regardless of the outcome, each interview is a stepping stone in your professional journey, providing lessons that enhance your confidence and competence. Engage with these experiences fully, knowing that authenticity is your strongest ally in navigating the complex world of interviews.

3.6 Entrepreneurship and Self-Employment: Creating Your Niche

Imagine standing at the crossroads of innovation and opportunity, where the traditional career paths diverge, giving way to the vast expanse of entrepreneurial ventures. This realm promises autonomy, creativity, and the chance to build something remarkable. For many autistic individuals, entrepreneurship is not just an alternative career path but a canvas to paint their unique vision of success. It begins with identifying gaps in the market—those unmet needs or overlooked opportunities that, once recognized, can be transformed into thriving businesses. The journey of successful autistic entrepreneurs is a testament to the boundless potential that exists when one dares to think beyond conventional frameworks. Their stories, rich with ingenuity and resilience, serve as both inspiration and blueprint for those seeking to carve their entrepreneurial niche.

Building a business plan is akin to constructing the blueprint of a dream, meticulously detailing each component that will bring your vision to life. At the heart of this process lies the value proposition—a compelling statement articulating your business's unique benefits to its customers. It is the promise of value that consumers choose your product or service over the available options. Yet, a compelling value proposition is the beginning; financial planning and budgeting are the foundational pillars supporting your entrepreneurial endeavor. This involves forecasting expenses, estimating revenue streams, and ensuring that you have the necessary capital to sustain your operations in the early stages. You lay the groundwork for an innovative and financially viable venture by approaching financial planning with rigor and foresight.

The path of self-employment is not without its challenges; each hurdle tests your determination and adaptability. Managing work-life balance as an entrepreneur is a delicate dance, where the boundaries between personal and professional often blur. It requires a conscious effort to delineate time for work from time for rest and recreation, ensuring that neither sphere is neglected. Strategies for maintaining motivation and discipline are essential, as the freedom of entrepreneurship can sometimes lead to procrastination or burnout. Consider setting regular goals, creating a structured schedule, and celebrating small victories. These practices can help sustain momentum, keeping you focused and driven even in adversity.

Leveraging unique strengths in business is a powerful way to differentiate your venture in a crowded market. As an entrepreneur, you can infuse your business with your personal values, creating a brand that resonates with authenticity and purpose. This alignment between business and values attracts like-minded customers and fosters a sense of fulfillment and satisfaction in your work. Building a business model around your inherent strengths allows you to capitalize on what you do best: problem-solving, creative thinking, or meticulous attention to detail. This synergy between personal and professional transforms your business from a mere enterprise into a reflection of your identity and aspirations.

3.7 Autism Across Cultures: Understanding Global Perspectives

The tapestry of cultural perceptions of autism is as varied and intricate as the world itself. Each culture brings beliefs and misconceptions that shape how autism is understood and responded to. In some societies, traditional beliefs may see autism through a lens of superstition or stigma, attributing it to spiritual or moral failings. These perspectives can lead to marginalization, as individuals on the spectrum are often misunderstood or ostracized. In contrast, other cultures might embrace neurodiversity, recognizing the unique contributions that autistic individuals can make. Media plays a pivotal role in shaping these perceptions, influencing public opinion by portraying autistic characters. While some media representations are sensitive and accurate, others can perpetuate stereotypes, reinforcing misconceptions and hindering acceptance. Understanding these cultural narratives is crucial for advocating effectively and fostering a more inclusive global community.

Cultural views have a profound impact on the lives of autistic individuals, affecting everything from social acceptance to access to critical resources. In regions where stigma prevails, autistic individuals may face significant barriers to education, employment, and healthcare, limiting their opportunities for growth and fulfillment. These environments can exacerbate feelings of isolation and diminish self-esteem, hindering individuals from reaching their potential. Conversely, cultures that embrace diversity and promote inclusion provide a fertile ground for autistic individuals to thrive, offering support systems and opportunities that enhance their quality of life. The level of acceptance within a society often dictates the availability of resources, from specialized educational programs to workplace accommodations. Advocating for greater awareness and understanding can help shift cultural perceptions, paving the way for more supportive environments that empower autistic individuals to succeed.

Examining how autism is approached in different regions reveals a landscape marked by progress and disparity. Developed countries may have well-established policies and support systems, providing frameworks for inclusion and accommodation in various sectors. These policies often result from years of advocacy and collaboration among stakeholders, leading to a more informed and supportive approach to autism. In contrast, developing countries may struggle with limited resources and infrastructure, impacting their ability to provide adequate support. However, innovative cultural initiatives in these regions demonstrate resilience and creativity, finding ways to support autistic individuals despite systemic challenges. Community-based programs, often driven by grassroots efforts, highlight the power of local advocacy and the potential for meaningful change. We can learn from these diverse approaches by sharing knowledge and strategies across borders, fostering a more unified and effective global response to autism.

Global perspectives offer invaluable lessons and strategies that can be adopted to enhance advocacy and support for autistic individuals. Successful international campaigns highlight the importance of collaboration and communication, bringing together voices across the spectrum to advocate for change. These campaigns often leverage storytelling to convey powerful messages, using personal narratives to build empathy and understanding. Community-based support models, which prioritize the needs and strengths of individuals, provide a blueprint for creating inclusive environments that celebrate diversity. By embracing these models, we can cultivate communities that accommodate and empower autistic individuals, recognizing their potential and contributions. The exchange of ideas and experiences between cultures enriches our understanding of autism, enabling us to create more inclusive societies where everyone can thrive.

3.8 Navigating Cultural Nuances: Embracing Diversity in Neurodiversity

Understanding cultural nuances in neurodiversity is akin to learning a new language, where the words and gestures hold different meanings across borders. Language differences can shape how autism is perceived and discussed, influencing personal and societal attitudes. For example, some cultures may use terms that emphasize disability, whereas others might focus on capability and potential. Depending on the cultural context, this linguistic variance can perpetuate stigma or foster acceptance. Moreover, cultural attitudes towards disability vary significantly, affecting the support systems available to autistic individuals. In some societies, disability may be viewed through a lens of charity, eliciting pity rather than empowerment, while others may celebrate neurodiversity as an integral part of human complexity. Understanding these nuanced cultural attitudes is crucial for effective communication and advocacy, allowing us to tailor our strategies to resonate with diverse audiences.

Embracing diversity within neurodiversity requires an appreciation for the kaleidoscope of experiences that autistic individuals bring. Celebrating cultural traditions and practices is one way to honor this diversity, recognizing that each individual's background enriches their perspective and contributions. Sharing diverse personal stories of autistic individuals can illuminate how people navigate their lives, offering insights that challenge stereotypes and expand our understanding of what it means to be autistic. These narratives, drawn from different cultural contexts, reveal the resilience and adaptability inherent in the human spirit, inspiring others to embrace their unique identities. By valuing these stories, we cultivate a culture of inclusion and respect, where differences are seen not as barriers but as opportunities for connection and growth.

Adapting communication to cultural contexts is essential in bridging the gaps that language and cultural differences can create. Techniques for overcoming language barriers include using clear, simple language and avoiding idiomatic expressions that may not translate well across cultures. Visual aids, such as diagrams or illustrations, can also facilitate understanding, providing a universal language that transcends words. Culturally appropriate communication styles vary; some cultures value directness, while others prefer a more indirect approach. Being mindful of these preferences can enhance communication and foster mutual respect. Engaging in active listening, where you attentively hear and reflect on what is being communicated, can further strengthen cross-cultural interactions, demonstrating empathy and openness to diverse perspectives.

Building cultural competence is an ongoing journey that enriches personal and professional interactions. Participating in cultural sensitivity training offers a structured approach to understanding the intricacies of cultural diversity, providing tools and insights that can inform your behavior and communication. These programs often explore unconscious bias, cultural norms, and effective cross-cultural communication, equipping you with the knowledge to navigate diverse environments confidently. Engaging with multicultural communities through community events or online platforms further enhances cultural competence, allowing you to experience the richness of diverse cultures firsthand. These interactions offer opportunities to learn from others, share your thoughts, emotions, and actions, and build meaningful connections across cultural boundaries. By fostering cultural competence, you enhance your understanding of the world and create more inclusive and harmonious communities where diversity is celebrated and valued.

3.9 Inclusive Workplaces: Fostering Respect and Understanding

Creating an inclusive work environment demands more than just policies on paper; it requires a cultural shift that embraces diversity as a core value. Implementing diversity and inclusion policies is foundational, yet their effectiveness hinges on how deeply they are integrated into the everyday fabric of workplace life. These policies must be living documents, adaptable to the evolving needs of the workforce, and should actively promote the benefits of a diverse team. Encouraging open dialogue about differences is crucial in this endeavor. When employees feel safe to express their identities and experiences, it fosters a culture of respect and understanding. Regular forums or discussions can serve as platforms for these exchanges, where employees are invited to share their perspectives and listen to others, thereby cultivating an environment where diversity is tolerated and celebrated. Such openness enhances interpersonal relationships and drives innovation as diverse ideas and approaches are presented.

Inclusivity training is indispensable in embedding these values within an organization. Designing autism awareness workshops is particularly impactful, as they educate employees about the spectrum of experiences within the autistic community, dispelling myths and fostering empathy. These workshops should be interactive, engaging participants in scenarios challenging preconceived notions and encouraging empathetic understanding. Additionally, developing cultural competency training for employees is essential in equipping teams to navigate the complexities of a multicultural workforce. These training sessions should focus on recognizing and respecting cultural differences, understanding unconscious biases, and learning effective communication strategies that transcend cultural barriers. By investing in these educational initiatives, organizations enhance their inclusivity and empower employees with the skills to thrive in a diverse world.

Despite these efforts, challenges persist, particularly for autistic individuals who may encounter microaggressions or subtle biases in the workplace. Addressing these issues requires a proactive approach, where strategies for dealing with microaggressions are openly discussed and implemented. Encouraging employees to speak up when they witness such behaviors and providing a precise mechanism for reporting and addressing them is vital in creating a safe and supportive environment. Furthermore, advocating for inclusive workplace practices goes beyond addressing negative behaviors; it involves creating pathways for success for all employees, regardless of their neurodiversity. This might include establishing mentorship programs or peer support groups that provide guidance and encouragement, helping individuals navigate their unique challenges. By fostering a workplace culture that actively supports diversity, organizations can ensure that all employees feel valued and empowered to contribute their best work.

At the heart of these efforts lies the role of respect in building inclusive workplaces. Creating inclusive language guidelines is one way to promote respectful communication, ensuring that language used within the organization is considerate and inclusive of all identities. These guidelines should be developed collaboratively, with input from diverse employee groups, to ensure they reflect the experiences and needs of the workforce. Encouraging peer support and mentorship programs further strengthens the culture of respect, providing opportunities for employees to learn from one another and build lasting connections. By pairing individuals from different backgrounds or experiences, these programs facilitate the exchange of knowledge and perspectives, fostering mutual respect and understanding. As these relationships develop, they contribute to a workplace where diversity is acknowledged and seen as a source of strength and enrichment.

Creating an inclusive workplace is an ongoing commitment, one that requires continuous effort and reflection. It involves implementing policies and training and fostering a culture where everyone feels seen, heard, and respected. Through these efforts, organizations can cultivate environments where diversity thrives, unlocking the full potential of their workforce and driving innovation and success.

3.10 Advocacy in Diverse Communities: Creating Impactful Change

Understanding the dynamics of a community is akin to deciphering a complex tapestry, where each thread represents unique influences and powers shaping the broader narrative. Recognizing key stakeholders and influencers within these networks becomes paramount when engaging in advocacy. These individuals or groups wield significant influence, capable of swaying public opinion or policy. They might include local leaders, influential community members, or organizations already active in the field. Equally important is an awareness of cultural power structures, those implicit hierarchies that dictate who holds sway and whose voices are amplified. Navigating these structures requires tact and insight, ensuring that your advocacy efforts resonate authentically and constructively within the community. By acknowledging and engaging with these dynamics, you position yourself to effect meaningful change, aligning your efforts with the community's values and priorities.

Crafting advocacy strategies that resonate across diverse audiences involves a nuanced approach that tailors messages to reflect each group's unique cultural and social contexts. Storytelling, a powerful vehicle for conveying complex ideas, becomes essential in this process. Stories have the power to transcend barriers, evoking empathy and understanding where statistics and facts alone may falter. You create a compelling tapestry that invites engagement and action by integrating personal narratives with broader advocacy goals. This approach humanizes the cause and allows individuals to see themselves reflected in the narrative, fostering a deeper connection to the mission. Tailoring these stories to align with the values and experiences of your audience ensures that your message is both relevant and impactful, encouraging active participation and support.

Building coalitions and alliances amplifies the reach and effectiveness of advocacy efforts, transforming solitary voices into a harmonious chorus of change. Partnering with local organizations and leaders can provide invaluable insights and resources, facilitating a more coordinated and cohesive approach to advocacy. These partnerships leverage the strengths and networks of each participant, creating a synergy that enhances the overall impact of your initiatives. Forming multicultural advocacy groups further enriches this collaborative effort, bringing together diverse perspectives and experiences that inform and refine your strategies. This collective approach strengthens the advocacy movement and fosters a sense of unity and shared purpose, empowering communities to address challenges and pursue opportunities with renewed vigor.

Measuring the impact of advocacy efforts is crucial in ensuring that your initiatives are effective and sustainable. Setting measurable goals provides a clear framework for assessing progress, allowing you to track the tangible outcomes of your campaigns. These goals should be specific, realistic, and aligned with the overarching mission of your advocacy work. Collecting and analyzing feedback from community members offers additional insights into the effectiveness of your strategies, highlighting areas of success and opportunities for improvement. This feedback loop ensures that your advocacy efforts remain responsive and adaptive, evolving in response to the needs and priorities of the community. By continually assessing and refining your approach, you ensure that your advocacy remains relevant and impactful, driving meaningful change in the lives of those you seek to support.

3.11 Building Inclusive Networks: Strength through Diversity

Inclusive networks are dynamic ecosystems where diverse perspectives converge, sparking innovation and fostering resilience through collaboration. Their role in promoting diversity is pivotal, offering platforms for exchanging ideas, experiences, and resources that enrich collective understanding. By encouraging cross-cultural dialogue and collaboration, these networks broaden their reach and amplify their impact, inviting participants to engage with perspectives beyond their own. This diversity of thought fuels creativity and enhances problem-solving, enabling a more holistic approach to complex challenges. In valuing and respecting differences, inclusive networks become potent catalysts for progress, achieving outcomes that homogeneous groups cannot.

Building and sustaining such networks requires intentional effort and strategic engagement. They do not form organically but evolve through purposeful actions, such as hosting multicultural networking events that create opportunities for diverse individuals to connect, share, and collaborate. These events should foster open dialogue and meaningful virtual or in-person interactions. Additionally, leveraging social media platforms extends the network's reach globally, enabling individuals to engage with peers and thought leaders from different cultures. By transcending geographic boundaries, digital platforms cultivate a global community united by shared values and goals, enriching the network's capacity to address complex global issues.

Active engagement is key to sustaining inclusive networks. Without ongoing interaction, networks risk stagnation and loss of relevance. Regular communication, such as newsletters, virtual meetups, or online forums, keeps members informed and connected, fostering a sense of belonging. Collaborative projects strengthen relationships by aligning members toward common goals, enhancing the network's impact and individual contributions. Such initiatives empower participants to leverage their unique skills and perspectives, resulting in more prosperous, more effective outcomes. Through consistent engagement and collaboration, inclusive networks remain vibrant, adaptive, and attuned to the evolving needs of their members and communities.

Inclusive networks hold immense potential for driving meaningful social change. Mobilizing them for advocacy and awareness campaigns amplifies their influence, transforming localized initiatives into movements that resonate on a broader scale. These campaigns can harness the power of storytelling to build empathy and understanding, highlighting the unique experiences of network members. Furthermore, channeling network resources into community initiatives can address systemic challenges through coordinated action, creating tangible improvements in the lives of those they serve. These efforts, propelled by the passion and commitment of diverse members, not only foster individual growth but also help build more inclusive societies where diversity is celebrated as a source of strength.

Inclusive networks emerge as essential conduits for fostering innovation and collaboration in the intricate weave of professional and social landscapes. They represent a vibrant marketplace of ideas where diverse voices contribute unique insights to shared challenges. By cultivating intentional, inclusive spaces—both online and offline—we unlock the power of diversity to fuel creativity and solve problems with multifaceted strategies. As these networks grow and evolve, they stand as beacons of progress, inspiring individuals and communities to join forces in pursuit of a more equitable and inclusive future.

3.12 Cultural Sensitivity: Navigating Global Differences

In our interconnected world, cultural sensitivity isn't just a noble ideal but a necessary skill for meaningful global interactions. Respecting cultural norms and traditions is paramount, as these threads weave the rich tapestry of human experience. Imagine stepping into a room where each person carries a unique set of customs and beliefs—understanding and honoring these differences can transform a simple interaction into a profound connection. Avoiding cultural stereotypes and assumptions is equally vital. These oversimplified views often obscure the depth and diversity inherent in every culture, leading to miscommunication and missed opportunities for understanding. When we approach each interaction with an open mind and a willingness to learn, we foster environments where diverse perspectives are valued and celebrated.

Adopting culturally sensitive practices involves more than just awareness; it requires a deliberate effort to incorporate cultural perspectives into decision-making processes. This means actively seeking out and considering viewpoints that may differ from your own, ensuring that decisions are informed by a holistic understanding of the cultural context. Engaging in active listening and empathy is crucial in this endeavor. By truly listening, we allow ourselves to see the world through another's eyes, acknowledging their experiences and emotions without judgment. Empathy bridges the gap between our perspective and that of others, fostering a deeper connection and understanding that transcends cultural boundaries.

In professional settings, navigating global differences demands adaptability and nuance. Leadership styles must often be tailored to accommodate diverse teams, recognizing that what motivates one group may not resonate with another. This flexibility is not a compromise but an enhancement, allowing leaders to draw on the strengths of their team members and create an inclusive atmosphere. Managing cross-cultural conflict resolution is another critical aspect. Conflicts can arise from misunderstandings or differing expectations, and resolving them requires a sensitive approach that respects all parties involved. By facilitating open dialogue and seeking common ground, you can transform potential discord into opportunities for collaboration and growth.

Promoting global inclusivity is an ongoing commitment that extends beyond the confines of any single organization. Advocating for international inclusion standards ensures that diversity is not just acknowledged but actively embraced at all levels. Participation in global inclusivity forums and events provides a platform for sharing best practices, learning from others, and building networks that transcend borders. These gatherings are fertile ground for innovation, where new ideas and approaches can be exchanged and refined. By engaging in these efforts, you contribute to a broader movement towards a world where inclusivity is the norm, not the exception.

As we conclude this chapter, consider how cultural sensitivity and global inclusivity can enrich personal and professional realms, setting the stage for the next exploration of continuous improvement and lifelong success.

Book 4: The Book of Continuous Improvement and Lifelong Success

Imagine a world where the definition of "normal" is as diverse as the people who inhabit it, where your unique ways of thinking and being are celebrated as the norm rather than the exception. As autistic adults and neurodivergent individuals, we often find ourselves at odds with societal expectations that insist on conformity and homogeneity. These expectations can manifest in myriad ways—the prescriptive career paths we are encouraged to pursue, the social behaviors we are expected to emulate, or the acceptable lifestyle choices. Too often, these societal norms serve as invisible shackles, constraining our authentic selves and stifling our potential. It is time to challenge these traditional norms and redefine "normal" on our own terms, embracing a mindset prioritizing personal fulfillment over societal approval.

Consider the social assumption that success relates to climbing a company ladder or accomplishing specific product turning points. Such slim meanings of success can be specifically restricting people who see the world with a different lens, which values depth and credibility over surface success.

Accepting a change in thinking in the direction of individual gratification implies turning down these personalized stories and creating a course that aligns with your values and enthusiasm.

This requires reflection and nerve. Unburdened by outside judgments, check out the passions and enthusiasms that fire up your spirit. Take time to journal your ideas, assessing what brings you delight and complete satisfaction. Consider motivators such as, "What activities make me lose track of time?" or "How do I feel most alive?" These reflections can serve as a compass, guiding you toward a life that resonates with your authentic self.

Credibility frequently requires susceptibility, an ability to share your authentic self with the world despite the threats of judgment or false impressions. Confessing susceptibility can be an effective stimulant for much deeper links and self-acceptance, enabling you to lose the facade of uniformity and welcome the liberty of being unapologetically you. Share your tales with trusted pals who can use assistance and understanding without judgment.

These stories confirm your experiences, grow affection and count on enhancing the bonds that link us as human beings. Participate in tasks that align with your individual worth, whether offering for a reason you're enthusiastic about or seeking a pastime that meets you. These activities strengthen your dedication to credibility, permitting you to reside in consistency with your internal reality.

To live genuinely is to carry out a constant procedure of self-discovery and development that develops as you do.

Establishing an individual credibility strategy can provide a structured plan for this recurring trip, supplying clarity and instructions. Start by establishing objectives for your day-to-day activities and aligning them with your core values and ambitions. Develop a dream board—a motivating aesthetic depiction of your goals and desires- to suggest your dedication to credibility. Consistently evaluate and readjust your strategy, enabling versatility, adjustment, brand-new understandings, and experiences that form your knowledge.

This strategy is not a stiff plan but a living document that develops with you, mirroring your continuous journey toward self-discovery and credibility.

4.1 Interactive Element: Craft Your Dream Board

Collect products such as publications, pictures, or online pictures that reverberate with your vision of credibility. Produce a collection that represents your worth, interests, and ambitions. Position your dream board in a noticeable area and review it consistently to assess your development and readjust your intent as needed.

I have my Dream Board in my bedroom and a copy, always colorful, in my office. My recommendation is to look at least twice a day: when you wake up and when you go to sleep. With your fixed eyes on it, create your I AM, I HAVE, and I CAN statement, and repeat it while visualizing your Dream Board. I will give you my statement as an example, feel free to create your own using mine as a reference. Every single time I look at my Dream Board, I say to myself: I am the son of God,

I have special, unique skills, and I can love myself as I love my neighbors.

Keep your board always updated, adding new dreams and taking out with celebration the ones you conquered; for instance, this book you are reading right now had its picture on my Dream Board.

In this technique of living, remember that the objective is not to attain a fixed state of being but to welcome a vibrant together with an advancing procedure of self-discovery. As you test social standards and redefine "normal" by their terms, you open the door to a life that is distinctively your own, loaded with opportunities and satisfaction. Allow your credibility to be a sign that overviews you with the intricacies of life, brightening the course in the direction of a future where your authentic self can thrive.

4.2 Setting Goals for Lifelong Success: A Roadmap for Growth

Life without objectives is similar to readying without a location- adrift, prone to every moving event, and prone to passing tornadoes. Objectives give the framework, inspiration, and instructions essential to browsing the intricacies of life, particularly for those who prosper on clarity and function. They work as signs assisting us with the haze of unpredictability, brightening the course for individual and specialist success. By establishing clear, possible objectives, you develop a guidebook that streamlines decision-making and encourages you to conquer barriers and gas your energy towards long-lasting success.

It is crucial to compare temporary and long-lasting goals; the former provide prompt targets to keep you involved and inspired, while the latter form your overarching vision and are particularly aligned with your values and desires. Together, they create a natural structure that sustains constant development and satisfaction.

The SMART framework—an acronym for Specific, Measurable, Achievable, Relevant, and Time-bound—is an effective device for crafting achievable and impactful objectives. This technique transforms unclear ambitions into concrete strategies, giving them clarity and emphasis.

Consider the distinction between a single objective like "get fit" and a SMART objective such as "lose 10 extra pounds in 3 months by working out three times per week and adhering to a well-balanced diet". The last is not just particular and quantifiable but additionally bound by a duration, making it extra workable and less complicated to track. To use this structure to your individual and expert desires, participate in workouts that test you to specify your objectives accurately. Assess what genuinely matters to you, coupled with expressing your goals in such a way that accompanies your strengths and conditions.

Tracking progress toward your objectives is essential to success, guaranteeing that you continue to be answerable and inspired. Digital devices like Trello or Notion can act as crucial allies in this venture, using user-friendly systems for objective monitoring. These devices permit you to arrange your goals, break them down into convenient jobs, and check your improvement gradually.

Establishing routine testimonial days is similarly crucial. These days allow you to analyze your development, commemorate success, and recalibrate your technique if necessary.

This step-by-step procedure promotes flexibility, ensuring that your objectives remain appropriate and aligned with your progressing conditions.

Despite our best intentions, goal-setting is typically filled with obstacles, from laziness to unanticipated life adjustments that require a change in concerns. Laziness that stealthily burglars time and efficiency can be attended to by damaging objectives right into smaller-sized, extra convenient jobs, minimizing the bewilder that commonly activates evasion. Developing a regular that integrates usual progression checks can assist in preserving emphasis as well as energy.

Yet life is uncertain, and scenarios might develop that require you to readjust your objectives. Instead of seeing these modifications as obstacles, see them as chances to fine-tune your purposes and guarantee they proceed to serve your best interests. Accept adaptability, understanding that the capability to adjust is a toughness that boosts your durability and the ability for development.

Participating in these approaches improves one's capacity to establish and accomplish purposeful objectives and encourages one to live a life abundant in function and satisfaction.

As you explore the ins and outs of goal-setting, remember that the journey is as crucial as the destination, offering numerous possibilities for understanding, development, and self-discovery.

4.3 Harnessing Creativity and Innovation: Unleashing Your Potential

Creative thinking is the keystone of development, a crucial component that fuels individual and expert growth. The stimulus stirs up development, driving us to test the standard and visualize opportunities past the traditional.

In a world that commonly values uniformity, welcoming imaginative reasoning is a radical act that encourages you to examine originalities and viewpoints. Methods include conceptualizing work as effective stimulants for imagination and using a free-flowing area where suggestions can arise and develop regardless of how non-traditional.

Urging varied viewpoints is just as vital. By welcoming input from people with different experiences and perspectives, you can cultivate a setting where imagination prospers. This variety of assumptions improves the imaginative procedure and results in much more cutting-edge and efficient options, simplifying and opening up brand-new opportunities for success.

Like creative thinking, advancement is a vibrant pressure that drives development and opens doors to new possibilities. It is the engine that thrusts markets ahead, changing difficulties right into success. Consider the modern technology field, where businesses like SAP and Microsoft have dreamt up human resources techniques to include neurodiverse skills, boosting efficiency and advancement, as noted in the Harvard Business Review. These studies show how welcoming development can result in cutting-edge improvements and one-upmanship on the market.

Ingenious problem-solving methods, such as layout reasoning, supply organized strategies for taking on intricate obstacles, allowing you to come close to troubles with imagination coupled with critical insight.

By seeing barriers as possibilities for advancement, you promote a state of mind that welcomes modification and leverages it for development and improvement.

To support imagination, developing a physical and psychological environment that influences and promotes it is crucial. Creating a work environment that contributes to creative thinking entails more than looks; it needs an atmosphere that urges expedition and trial and error.

Consider natural illumination, open formats, and adaptable seating plans that advertise convenience and adaptability. Including breaks with recreation into your regimen is just as vital as they supply the psychological space required for ideas to hatch and thrive. Tasks such as strolling, contemplating, or participating in a pastime can stimulate ideas, permitting your mind to stray and discover brand-new opportunities. This equilibrium between structured jobs and leisure cultivates an innovative setting where technology can grow.

In the electronic age, modern technology plays a critical duty in boosting imagination, using devices and systems that equip you to bring your suggestions to life.

Digital mapping and layout devices such as Adobe Creative Suite or Procreate supply functional canvases for imagining ideas and exploring brand-new styles. These devices allow you to explore innovative suggestions without the restrictions of standard tools, permitting better adaptability and technology. Efficiency applications like Obsidian, frequently described as a 'second brain,' provide a vibrant system for arranging ideas, managing jobs, and recording motivation.

These technical sources can enhance processes, improve cooperation, and magnify your imaginative capacity. Accepting innovation not only boosts your capability to introduce but likewise furnishes you with the devices required to navigate the intricacies of modern-day life with imagination and self-confidence.

4.4 Practical Tools for Personal and Professional Development

Recognizing areas for personal and professional development begins with a keen eye toward introspection. It requires the courage to conduct self-assessments that reveal skill gaps and areas ripe for improvement. This process is akin to tuning an instrument, where each adjustment brings greater harmony and clarity to one's capabilities. Self-assessment can be facilitated through introspective exercises or structured tools that highlight strengths while also identifying areas for growth. Seeking feedback from mentors and peers provides an external perspective that is invaluable in this endeavor. These individuals, who understand your goals and challenges, offer insights that can illuminate blind spots, offering constructive criticism that propels you forward. Engaging in open dialogue with those who support your aspirations creates a feedback loop that nurtures development, ensuring that growth is both intentional and informed.

The digital era has ushered in a wealth of opportunities for continuous learning, making education more accessible than ever before. Online learning platforms such as Coursera, Udemy, and LinkedIn Learning provide a cornucopia of courses across a myriad of disciplines tailored to suit diverse learning styles and goals. These platforms offer the flexibility to learn at your own pace, accommodating the unique schedules and preferences of neurodivergent individuals. When selecting courses, consider your long-term objectives and the skills you wish to acquire or enhance. Evaluate course content, instructor credentials, and reviews to ensure alignment with your goals. The ability to curate a personalized curriculum empowers you to chart a course that is as unique as your aspirations, fostering a sense of agency and excitement in the pursuit of knowledge.

Integrating learning into daily life requires a deliberate approach that balances demands with the desire for growth. Scheduling regular "learning hours" each week creates a structured routine that prioritizes education, transforming it from a sporadic activity into a consistent practice. Consider dedicating specific times each day or week to engage with educational content, whether through reading, online courses, or interactive workshops. For those with busy schedules, podcasts and audiobooks provide an excellent medium for on-the-go learning, allowing you to absorb new information during commutes or daily chores. These resources, which cover a vast array of topics, offer the flexibility to learn while carrying out everyday tasks, seamlessly integrating education into your lifestyle. This multifaceted approach to learning ensures that personal and professional development remains at the forefront, a constant thread woven into the fabric of your daily existence.

Evaluating progress is a critical component of personal and professional development, as it ensures that learning efforts yield meaningful results. Establishing benchmarks for skill acquisition provides tangible targets to strive toward, offering a precise measure of success. These benchmarks, whether they involve mastering a new technology, enhancing communication skills, or achieving a professional certification, serve as milestones that mark progress and motivate continued effort. Regularly assess your advancement against these benchmarks, celebrating achievements and identifying areas where further improvement is needed. Adjusting learning plans based on progress and feedback is an iterative process, one that demands flexibility and an openness to change. This adaptability, in response to both successes and setbacks, ensures that your development journey remains dynamic and responsive to your evolving goals and circumstances, allowing you to thrive in both personal and professional arenas.

4.5 Leading Change: Inspiring Others with Your Unique Perspective

True leadership, particularly for those of us who identify as autistic adults or neurodivergent, is about summoning the courage to step into the role of a change leader. This calls for comprehending that leading adjustment does not involve utilizing power but instead motivating others via credibility and vision. Efficient modification leaders personify attributes that speak deeply with those they lead; they are compassionate, resistant, and dedicated to growing settings where everyone feels valued.

They lead not via browbeating but through instance, inspiring their groups and neighborhoods with a real enthusiasm for development and addition. Genuine management produces surges of favorable effect, motivating those around us to welcome their distinct point of view and add purposefully. This technique equips people and grows a society of count on and collaboration, vital for driving lasting adjustment.

Interacting vision and function is the lifeline of management, a necessary ability that can galvanize groups and areas toward a common objective.

An engaging story is an effective device in this undertaking, weaving with each other the strings of function and instructions in such a way that reverberates with varied target markets. Crafting these stories is more significant than words; it needs an understanding of the worths and goals of those you seek to motivate. Narration is a considerable tool right here as it links to a psychological degree, going beyond obstacles and promoting a feeling of ordinary trip and function. By sharing individual stories and experiences, you can show the effect of modification in relatable terms, inspiring interest and dedication in those you lead. This touch humanizes the vision, making it a substantial plus possible for all.

Producing a change-ready society is essential for any neighborhood or company, making every effort to adjust and thrive in an ever-changing world. This includes supporting an atmosphere where open-mindedness and versatility are not simply urged but commemorated. Urging employees to articulate their concepts and points of view, regardless of how non-traditional, promotes a society of advancement and inclusivity.

Commending tiny successes along the course to more significant objectives can construct energy and maintain the spirit, enhancing the idea that progression is feasible and possible. Identifying the initiatives and payments of people at every degree not only encourages but also grows a feeling of possession and financial investment in the adjustment procedure. By supporting flexibility plus commemorating success, you lay the groundwork for a society that invites modification as a possibility for development and advancement.

Empowering others to lead is one of the most impactful acts of leadership. It involves recognizing the potential in others and providing them with the tools and opportunities to step into leadership roles themselves. Mentoring and coaching emerging leaders is a crucial component of this empowerment, offering guidance and support as they navigate their leadership journeys. By sharing your experiences and insights, you can help them develop the skills and confidence needed to lead effectively. Creating opportunities for team members to lead projects or initiatives not only builds their leadership capabilities but also fosters a sense of ownership and responsibility. This empowerment extends beyond individual growth; it strengthens the collective fabric of the organization or community, ensuring a legacy of leadership that is diverse, dynamic, and resilient.

In this exploration of leadership and change, the focus remains on the transformative power of authenticity, vision, and empowerment. As you lead change in your community or organization, remember that your unique perspective is a valuable asset, capable of inspiring others and effecting meaningful transformation. By embracing the role of a change leader, you not only contribute to the evolution of your environment but also pave the way for others to do the same, creating a ripple effect of positive change that extends far beyond your immediate sphere.

4.6 Building a Supportive Network: Community and Connection

In the intricate tapestry of personal and professional life, networks serve as the threads that connect and sustain us, providing the resources and support essential for growth and success. These networks act as a dynamic ecosystem, offering a rich array of opportunities and insights that can propel you forward in both personal and professional realms. The value of a supportive network cannot be overstated; it provides not only practical resources but also emotional sustenance, enhancing resilience and adaptability. It is crucial to differentiate between personal and professional networks, as each serves distinct yet complementary roles. Personal networks are those intimate circles of friends and family who offer unconditional support and understanding, while professional networks consist of colleagues, mentors, and industry peers who provide guidance, opportunities, and collaboration. Together, these networks form a robust framework that underpins personal fulfillment and professional achievement, enabling you to navigate the complexities of life with confidence and poise.

Cultivating meaningful connections within these networks requires intentionality and empathy, fostering relationships that are both genuine and supportive. Engaging in active listening is a foundational skill in this endeavor, as it demonstrates respect and attentiveness, allowing you to understand the perspectives and needs of others. By practicing empathy, you create an environment of trust and mutual understanding where connections are deepened, and collaboration is enhanced. Identifying common interests and goals is another key strategy, as it provides a shared foundation upon which relationships can be built and sustained. Whether through shared professional pursuits, common hobbies, or aligned values, these shared interests serve as the glue that binds connections, fostering a sense of belonging and camaraderie. By investing time and effort in cultivating these relationships, you not only enrich your network but also contribute to a culture of support and collaboration that benefits all involved.

Maintaining and expanding networks is a dynamic process that demands regular engagement and proactive communication. Techniques for regular check-ins and updates are vital in this regard, ensuring that relationships remain vibrant and reciprocal. Simple gestures, such as sending a message of appreciation or sharing relevant resources, can strengthen bonds and reinforce connections. Social media platforms, such as LinkedIn, offer powerful tools for professional networking, providing opportunities to connect with industry leaders, engage in discussions, and stay informed about trends and innovations. By leveraging these platforms, you can expand your network beyond geographic boundaries, accessing a global community of professionals who share your interests and aspirations. This proactive approach to networking not only sustains existing connections but also opens doors to new opportunities and collaborations, enriching both personal and professional landscapes.

Leveraging networks for personal and professional opportunities involves tapping into the wealth of knowledge and experience that resides within your connections. Seeking mentorship and advice from network connections is a particularly valuable practice, as it provides insights and guidance that can inform your decisions and strategies. Mentors, with their wealth of experience and perspective, offer invaluable support, helping you navigate challenges and seize opportunities. Collaborating on projects and initiatives with network members is another powerful way to leverage your connections, as it fosters innovation, creativity, and shared success. These collaborative efforts not only enhance your professional portfolio but also strengthen your relationships, reinforcing the bonds of trust and cooperation. By actively engaging with your networks, you create a dynamic and supportive environment that facilitates growth, learning, and achievement, empowering you to reach new heights in both personal and professional endeavors.

4.7 Embracing Change: Adaptability as a Strength

In the realm of personal and professional growth, adaptability emerges as a cornerstone of resilience, enabling individuals to navigate the ever-evolving landscape of life's challenges. The ability to adapt is akin to possessing a finely tuned compass, guiding you through the tumultuous seas of change with confidence and poise. The interconnection between adaptability and resilience is profound, as each supports and enhances the other, creating a dynamic synergy that fosters strength and stability. Consider the myriad industries that have been transformed by change—technology, healthcare, and education, to name a few. These sectors have thrived by embracing innovation and adaptability, demonstrating that flexibility is not merely a survival strategy but a catalyst for transformation and success.

Cultivating an adaptability mindset requires a conscious effort to remain open and receptive to new thoughts and emotions and take new actions. This involves practicing flexibility in everyday situations, whether it be altering your daily routine or approaching problems with a fresh perspective. By viewing challenges as opportunities for growth, you shift your mindset from one of resistance to one of curiosity and exploration. This shift invites you to embrace the unknown with a sense of wonder, transforming obstacles into stepping stones that propel you forward. Cultivating this mindset is an ongoing practice, one that requires patience and perseverance yet yields immeasurable rewards in the form of personal and professional growth.

Effectively implementing change in personal and professional contexts demands a strategic approach that balances planning with execution. This begins with a clear vision of the desired outcome, followed by a detailed plan that outlines the steps necessary to achieve it. Consider the importance of managing resistance and gaining buy-in from others, as change often elicits fear and uncertainty. By involving key stakeholders in the change process, you foster a sense of ownership and collaboration, ensuring that all voices are heard and valued. This collaborative approach not only mitigates resistance but also enhances the likelihood of success, as it leverages the collective wisdom and insights of those involved.

Reflecting on change outcomes is an invaluable practice that allows you to glean insights and lessons from your experiences. Conducting post-change evaluations provides an opportunity to assess the impact of the change, identifying areas of success and those in need of improvement. This reflective process invites you to celebrate achievements while also acknowledging setbacks, transforming them into valuable learning experiences. By identifying lessons learned, you equip yourself with the knowledge and insights needed to navigate future changes with greater confidence and effectiveness.

Seeking advice and mentorship is a powerful strategy for fostering growth and development, as it connects you with individuals who can offer guidance, support, and encouragement. Engaging with successful people who have navigated similar challenges provides you with a wealth of knowledge and inspiration, offering a roadmap for your own journey. Participating in business mentorship programs further enhances this process, providing structured opportunities for learning and growth. These programs not only connect you with experienced mentors but also create a supportive community of peers who share your aspirations and challenges. By actively seeking advice and mentorship, you empower yourself with the tools and insights needed to embrace change with confidence and resilience, ensuring that you remain adaptable and poised for success in both personal and professional endeavors.

4.8 Saving and Investing: Strategies for Long-Term Security

Financial literacy is a cornerstone of a well-lived life, particularly for those who seek independence and empowerment. Engaging in continuous learning about finance can be transformative, offering the knowledge and skills necessary to navigate the complexities of personal and professional financial landscapes. Consider participating in financial literacy courses, which provide structured insights into budgeting, investing, and financial planning. Books on personal finance can also serve as valuable resources, offering diverse perspectives and strategies tailored to different financial goals. Online platforms such as Coursera or Khan Academy offer courses that demystify the intricacies of finance, making it accessible to individuals across various backgrounds and experiences. By immersing yourself in these resources, you can build a solid foundation of financial knowledge, empowering you to make informed decisions that align with your goals, principles, and values.

Automating savings and investments is a powerful tool for ensuring consistent financial growth, reducing the temptation to spend impulsively. Setting up automatic transfers to a savings account can transform saving from a conscious effort into a seamless process, allowing your wealth to grow effortlessly over time. Consider establishing an emergency fund as a safety net, providing financial security and peace of mind in unforeseen circumstances. This fund acts as a buffer against life's uncertainties, ensuring that you are prepared for unexpected events without derailing your long-term financial goals. Additionally, automating contributions to retirement accounts or investment portfolios can further enhance economic security, allowing you to benefit from the power of compound interest over time. By leveraging technology to automate these processes, you can cultivate a disciplined approach to saving and investing, ensuring steady progress toward your financial aspirations.

Setting savings goals, both short-term and long-term, is integral to achieving financial stability and success. Short-term goals might include saving for a vacation, a new gadget, or even further education. These goals offer immediate targets to strive for, providing motivation and satisfaction as they are achieved. Long-term goals, on the other hand, require a more strategic approach, focusing on significant milestones such as home ownership, education, or retirement. By setting clear, achievable goals, you create a roadmap for your financial journey, offering direction and purpose. Consider using goal-setting frameworks, such as the SMART criteria, to define your objectives with precision. This approach ensures that your goals are specific, measurable, attainable, relevant, and time-bound, providing clarity and focus in your financial planning.

Understanding risk and diversification is crucial for effective investment management, allowing you to balance potential returns with the associated risks. Risk management involves assessing the level of risk you are comfortable with and tailoring your investment strategy accordingly. Diversification, the practice of spreading investments across various asset classes, is a key strategy for mitigating risk, ensuring that your portfolio remains resilient in fluctuating market conditions. By balancing high-risk and low-risk investments, you can achieve an optimal mix that aligns with your risk tolerance and financial goals. Exploring investment options involves understanding the different vehicles available, from stocks and bonds to mutual funds and real estate. Each offers unique benefits and risks, catering to diverse financial appetites and objectives. By educating yourself about these options, you can make informed decisions that maximize returns while minimizing exposure to unnecessary risk.

With these strategies in your financial toolkit, you are better equipped to navigate the complexities of saving and investing, ensuring long-term security and growth. The journey toward financial independence is not without its challenges, yet it is a path filled with opportunities for learning and empowerment. As you engage with these concepts, remember that the goal is not to achieve wealth for its own sake but to cultivate a financial foundation that supports your aspirations and values, enabling you to live a life of purpose and fulfillment.

4.9 Leading by Example: Inspiring Change in Your Community

Being a role model in the autism community requires authenticity and transparency, qualities that resonate deeply with those who seek guidance and inspiration. Authenticity involves being true to oneself, embracing both strengths and vulnerabilities and allowing others to see the genuine person behind the role. Transparency means sharing successes and challenges alike, offering a realistic portrayal of the journey towards self-discovery and empowerment. A commitment to continuous learning and growth is equally vital, as it demonstrates the willingness to evolve and adapt, qualities that inspire others to pursue their own paths of development. As a role model, your actions speak louder than words, and the values you embody can have a profound impact on those who look up to you.

Personal narratives hold immense power in inspiring others, providing a window into the lived experiences that shape who we are. By sharing your story at community events, you can offer insights and inspiration to others who may be navigating similar challenges. These stories, whether shared through public speaking or written articles and blogs, serve as beacons of hope and encouragement, illustrating the resilience and determination that define the autistic experience. They also challenge misconceptions and stereotypes, fostering greater understanding and acceptance within the broader community. Writing about your experiences allows you to connect with a wider audience, providing a platform for dialogue and exchange that can enrich both the storyteller and the listener.

Empowering others to take on leadership roles is a transformative act that amplifies your impact and fosters a culture of inclusivity and collaboration. Mentorship programs are a powerful tool in this regard, offering guidance and support to emerging leaders as they develop their skills and confidence. By serving as a mentor, you can share your knowledge and experiences, helping others navigate the challenges and opportunities of leadership. Providing support and resources for new initiatives also encourages others to step into leadership roles, fostering innovation and growth within the community. This empowerment is not only about passing the torch but also about creating a legacy of leadership that is diverse and dynamic, ensuring that the community continues to thrive and evolve.

Sustaining momentum in community initiatives requires both enthusiasm and strategic planning, ensuring that efforts remain vibrant and impactful. Celebrating small successes and milestones is a crucial aspect of this process, as it reinforces the value of progress and keeps motivation high. Acknowledging achievements, no matter how modest, fosters a sense of accomplishment and encourages continued effort. Continual innovation and adaptation of strategies are also essential, as they ensure that initiatives remain responsive to changing needs and circumstances. By embracing flexibility and creativity, you can develop approaches that are both effective and sustainable, ensuring that community efforts have a lasting impact.

The role of a leader in the autism community is multifaceted, encompassing authenticity, inspiration, empowerment, and sustainability. By leading by example, you can inspire change and foster a culture of inclusivity and growth, creating a community where everyone is valued and empowered to reach their full potential. This approach not only benefits individuals but also strengthens the community as a whole, creating a ripple effect of positive change that extends far beyond its immediate boundaries. The qualities and actions you embody as a leader can inspire others to step forward, creating a dynamic and resilient community that thrives on diversity and collaboration. Through your leadership, you have the power to shape the future, paving the way for a more inclusive and understanding society.

4.10 Collaborative Efforts: Strength in Numbers

When you consider collaboration, envision a tapestry woven from threads of diverse skills and perspectives, each contributing its unique hue to the collective masterpiece. Identifying potential collaborators begins with reaching out to individuals and organizations whose missions resonate with your own. Local non-profits can be invaluable partners, offering established networks and community insights that amplify your impact. Engage with like-minded community leaders who share your passion for advocacy and change; together, you can forge alliances that transcend individual capabilities. These partnerships often begin with a simple conversation, a meeting of minds that sparks the potential for joint ventures. Share your vision, listen to theirs, and explore the synergies that naturally emerge. By building these connections, you lay the groundwork for collaborative efforts that are both meaningful and impactful, leveraging collective strengths to achieve shared goals.

Creating collaborative projects involves more than pooling resources; it's about weaving together the strengths and insights of each participant to create something more significant than the sum of its parts. Joint events and workshops on autism awareness serve as platforms for education and engagement, inviting diverse voices to participate in a dialogue that challenges stereotypes and promotes understanding. Consider community outreach programs that offer educational resources to schools, workplaces, and public forums, fostering an environment of inclusion and acceptance. These initiatives require careful planning and execution, ensuring that each collaborator's strengths are maximized and that the project aligns with the collective mission. By focusing on shared values and objectives, you can create projects that not only raise awareness but also drive tangible change within the community, fostering a culture of collaboration and mutual support.

Effective communication is the cornerstone of successful collaboration, ensuring that all parties are aligned and informed throughout the process. Begin by clearly establishing roles and responsibilities and delineating each collaborator's contributions and expectations. This clarity prevents misunderstandings and ensures that everyone is working toward the same goals. Regular updates and check-ins are equally important, providing opportunities to address challenges, celebrate progress, and make necessary adjustments. These touchpoints foster a sense of accountability and transparency, reinforcing the trust essential to successful collaboration. Embrace open dialogue and encourage feedback, creating an environment where all voices are heard and valued. This inclusive approach not only enhances communication but also strengthens the collaborative bond, ensuring that the effort remains cohesive and focused.

Evaluating the success of collaborative initiatives requires a thoughtful approach that considers both quantitative and qualitative measures. Analyze participant feedback to gain insights into the impact of the project, identifying areas of success and opportunities for improvement. This feedback, gathered through surveys, interviews, or informal discussions, provides a valuable perspective on the project's effectiveness and relevance. Measure community engagement by assessing participation levels, media coverage, and social media interaction, offering a tangible gauge of the initiative's reach and influence. By reflecting on these outcomes, you can identify best practices and lessons learned, inform future collaborative efforts, and ensure continuous improvement. This evaluation process not only enhances the efficacy of individual projects but also contributes to a broader understanding of what makes collaboration successful, empowering you to build stronger, more impactful partnerships in the future.

4.11 Promoting Autism Awareness and Acceptance

Advocacy serves as a transformative force, a catalyst for awareness and acceptance. It is the process of championing a cause, and for those of us within the autism community, it carries the profound responsibility of reshaping perceptions and dismantling stereotypes. Advocacy is not simply about speaking up; it's about crafting narratives that resonate, challenge the status quo, and elevate understanding. By raising awareness, we illuminate the diverse experiences of autistic individuals, highlighting strengths and potential rather than focusing solely on challenges. This awareness is crucial in breaking down the barriers of misconception that have long constrained our community. Moreover, advocacy extends to influencing policies and public perception, striving for a societal shift where neurodiversity is embraced and celebrated as an integral part of the human tapestry.

Developing effective advocacy campaigns requires a strategic approach, one that begins with crafting clear and impactful messages. These messages must be concise yet powerful, capable of capturing attention and inspiring action. It's about finding the right words to convey the essence of our experiences and aspirations, translating them into narratives that evoke empathy and understanding. Utilizing various media channels amplifies these messages, extending their reach far beyond immediate circles. Social media platforms, blogs, podcasts, and even traditional media outlets offer diverse avenues for outreach, each with the potential to engage different audiences. By harnessing the power of these channels, we can create a dynamic dialogue that fosters awareness and acceptance on a broader scale, sparking conversations that lead to meaningful change.

Engagement with policymakers and influencers is a critical aspect of advocacy, as these individuals hold the power to enact policies and shape public opinion. Writing letters to local representatives is a direct and impactful way to voice concerns and propose changes, offering a personal perspective that can sway decision-making. Participating in or organizing advocacy events further amplifies this engagement, providing platforms for discourse and collaboration. These events bring together stakeholders from various sectors, creating opportunities to share insights, build alliances, and advocate for policies that support the autistic community. Through these efforts, we can influence the legislative landscape, ensuring that it reflects the needs and rights of neurodivergent individuals.

The success of advocacy efforts hinges on the ability to measure their impact, a task that requires both qualitative and quantitative approaches. Gathering data on changes in awareness is an essential component, as it provides tangible evidence of progress and areas for improvement. Surveys and feedback from community members and stakeholders offer valuable insights, capturing the nuances of perception and understanding that may not be immediately visible. This feedback serves as a compass, guiding future advocacy efforts and ensuring that they remain responsive to the community's evolving needs. By continuously evaluating advocacy initiatives, we can refine our strategies, adapt to changing contexts, and maximize our impact, ultimately fostering a more inclusive and accepting society for all individuals.

4.12 The Future of Neurodiversity: Paving the Way for New Generations

The concept of neurodiversity has undergone a significant evolution, gaining recognition and acceptance as an essential aspect of human variation. This shift reflects a growing understanding that neurological differences are not deficits but rather valuable contributions to the diversity of human thought and experience. As we look to the future, we see emerging trends in neurodiversity advocacy, trends that emphasize inclusivity, empowerment, and the celebration of individual strengths. These trends are driven by a collective commitment to dismantling barriers and fostering environments where neurodivergent individuals can thrive. The implications of this evolution are profound, offering the promise of a society where diversity is not merely tolerated but embraced as a source of strength and innovation.

Preparing the next generation for this future requires equipping them with the tools and knowledge necessary to advocate for themselves and others. Educational programs play a fundamental role in this preparation, providing young individuals with an understanding of neurodiversity and the skills to navigate a complex world. These programs encourage empathy, inclusivity, and self-advocacy, laying the foundation for a more accepting society. Youth leadership and empowerment initiatives further enhance this preparation, cultivating the confidence and skills needed to lead change. By fostering a sense of agency and responsibility, these initiatives empower young individuals to become advocates and allies, paving the way for a future where neurodiversity is celebrated and supported.

Innovative approaches to fostering inclusivity are emerging across various sectors, driven by a recognition of the value that neurodiverse individuals bring to the table. Technological advancements are playing a crucial role in this shift, offering tools and platforms that support communication, collaboration, and creativity. Inclusive policies in workplaces and educational institutions are also gaining traction, reflecting a commitment to creating environments where everyone can succeed. These policies acknowledge the unique needs and strengths of neurodivergent individuals, providing the accommodations and support necessary for them to reach their full potential. By embracing innovative approaches, we can create a future where inclusivity is the norm, not the exception.

Envisioning a neurodiverse future involves imagining a world where differences are not only accepted but celebrated as integral to the human experience. This vision encompasses potential societal changes that enhance understanding, collaboration, and innovation. It acknowledges the ongoing challenges that remain, recognizing that true inclusivity requires continuous effort and adaptation. Yet, it also highlights the opportunities for growth and progress, offering a roadmap for a future where neurodiversity is embraced as a source of strength and inspiration. As we work toward this vision, we are reminded of the power of collective action and the impact that each of us can have in shaping a more inclusive and understanding world.

Neurodiversity, once a concept relegated to the fringes of academic discourse, has gradually emerged as a pivotal paradigm shift in our understanding of human cognition. This evolution reflects a broader societal transition towards recognizing neurological differences not as deficiencies to be remedied but as variations that enrich the tapestry of human experience. The implications are profound as society begins to embrace neurodiversity with an open heart and mind, reshaping perceptions and dismantling long-held stereotypes. Emerging trends in neurodiversity advocacy are increasingly focused on inclusivity and empowerment, advocating for environments where diverse neurological profiles are celebrated for their unique contributions. This progressive movement, fueled by passionate advocates and allies, seeks to ensure that neurodivergent individuals are seen, heard, and valued in all spheres of life, paving the way for a future where diversity in thought and perception is recognized as a cornerstone of innovation and progress.

Equipping future generations with the tools for advocacy and acceptance requires a concerted effort to integrate neurodiversity into educational frameworks. Schools, as the crucibles of young minds, hold the potential to shape attitudes and foster understanding from an early age. Academic programs that emphasize empathy, inclusion, and the value of diverse perspectives are instrumental in cultivating a culture of acceptance and respect. By incorporating neurodiversity into curricula, schools can provide students with a nuanced understanding of neurological differences, preparing them to become advocates and allies in their communities. Youth leadership and empowerment initiatives further reinforce this preparation, offering platforms for young individuals to develop their voices and leadership skills. These initiatives, which often involve mentorship, workshops, and community engagement, empower young people to take ownership of their narratives, equipping them with the confidence and skills needed to advocate for themselves and others.

Innovative approaches to fostering inclusivity are gaining traction across various sectors, driven by a recognition of the immense value that neurodiverse individuals bring to the table. Technological advancements are at the forefront of this shift, offering tools and platforms that enhance communication, collaboration, and creativity. For instance, voice recognition software, sensory-friendly apps, and adaptive technologies are empowering neurodivergent individuals to engage with the world on their terms, breaking down barriers and enhancing accessibility. Inclusive policies in workplaces and educational institutions are also gaining momentum, reflecting a commitment to creating environments where everyone can thrive. These policies, which often involve accommodations, flexible work arrangements, and diversity training, acknowledge the unique needs and strengths of neurodivergent individuals, providing the support necessary for them to reach their full potential. By embracing these innovative approaches, sectors across the board can create a more inclusive and equitable landscape, one where diversity is not only accepted but actively sought after and celebrated.

Envisioning a neurodiverse future involves imagining a world where differences are not only accepted but embraced as integral to the human experience. This vision encompasses potential societal changes that enhance understanding, collaboration, and innovation. It acknowledges the ongoing challenges that remain, recognizing that true inclusivity requires continuous effort and adaptation. Yet, it also highlights the opportunities for growth and progress, offering a roadmap for a future where neurodiversity is embraced as a source of strength and inspiration. As we work toward this vision, we are reminded of the power of collective action and the impact that each of us can have in shaping a more inclusive and understanding world. In this way, the future of neurodiversity is not just a distant ideal but an achievable reality, one that promises a more prosperous, more vibrant society for generations to come.

4.13 Building a Legacy: Inspiring Others with Your Journey

Legacy is an evocative term, often conjuring images of grand achievements or monumental contributions. Yet, at its core, a legacy is deeply personal, a reflection of the impact you wish to leave on the world and the lives you touch. For those of us who navigate life through the lens of autism or neurodiversity, legacy can take on a unique dimension. It is about the stories we share, the barriers we break, and the pathways we forge for others. It is about being remembered not just for what we achieved but for how we inspired others to see the world through a different lens, fostering understanding and acceptance in every interaction.

To define what legacy means to you, consider the values and principles that guide your actions. Reflect on the aspects of your identity that you hold dear and wish to pass on to others. It may be your resilience in the face of adversity, your commitment to advocating for neurodiversity, or your dedication to personal growth and learning. These elements form the foundation of your legacy, shaping the narratives you create and the influence you exert on those around you. By aligning your actions with these values, you ensure that your legacy is authentic and meaningful, a true reflection of who you are and what you stand for.

Inspiring others with your journey involves sharing your experiences, both the triumphs and the challenges, with openness and vulnerability. Personal stories are powerful tools for connection, offering insights into the complexities of living as a neurodivergent individual. By sharing these narratives, whether through writing, speaking, or everyday interactions, you invite others to walk alongside you, to see the world from your perspective, and to appreciate the richness of neurodiversity. These stories challenge stereotypes, dispel misconceptions, and foster empathy, creating a ripple effect that extends far beyond your immediate circle. They inspire others to embrace their own uniqueness, to advocate for acceptance, and to contribute to a more inclusive society.

The legacy you build is not static; it evolves as you do, influenced by your growth and the people you encounter along the way. It is cultivated through the choices you make and the relationships you nurture, each interaction leaving an indelible mark in your life. Consider how you can inspire others not only through your accomplishments but also through your commitment to lifting others up, mentoring, and supporting those who follow in your footsteps. By empowering others to lead, you create a legacy of leadership that is dynamic and enduring, one that transcends individual achievements and contributes to the collective progress of the community.

As you contemplate your legacy, remember that it is not solely defined by big gestures or public accolades. It is found in the quiet moments of connection, the small acts of kindness, and the courage to be true to yourself in a world that often demands conformity. Your legacy is the sum of these moments, a testament to the impact you have on the lives you touch and the change you inspire. It is a reminder that each of us, regardless of our circumstances, has the power to leave a lasting impression, shape the narrative of neurodiversity, and pave the way for a future where all voices are heard and valued.

Conclusion

As we attract this equipping trip to a close, I want to assess the core motifs that have actually been woven with each phase of this guide: identification, social skills, career empowerment, and continuous improvement. This trip has actually had to do with welcoming that you are, recognizing the remarkable toughness that features being an adult autistic, and also using that toughness to establish your course to success. Throughout these pages, we have browsed the complex area of self-discovery, covering everything from understanding your neurodivergent identification to the functional approaches for prospering socially and skillfully.

Allow us to take a minute to take another look at the vital understandings from each phase.

We started with the expedition of identification along with self-confidence, where we dug into the transformative experience of a late autism medical diagnosis, motivating you to welcome your neurodiversity as a resource of toughness instead of restriction. After that, we relocated right into social abilities plus partnerships, furnishing you with devices to translate social hints and create purposeful links, all while handling social anxiety with poise and expertise.

In the world of expert development, we discovered the vital function of developing your unique strengths, promoting required work environment holiday accommodations, and the art of networking with excellence. We better analyzed how entrepreneurship might be a canvas for painting your vision of success and how social subtleties improve the tapestry of neurodiversity.

The last phases concentrated on continual improvement, where we talked about redefining normality, establishing attainable objectives, and promoting creative thinking and advancement as foundations of long-lasting success.

Reflecting on this trip, I hope you have discovered the methods and understandings offered below to be both informative and sensible. It's my genuine dream that these devices have geared you up for individual and specialist success, encouraging you to see your neurodivergent attributes as possessions. As you move forward, please remember that self-validation is the structure coupled with real empowerment.

Accept your distinctions, for they are your most considerable strength, permitting you to live distinctly and confidently.

Throughout this guide, whether participating in office jobs, creating networking and partnerships, or conquering individual objectives, allow your strengths to be your guiding light.

The journey of self-discovery is ongoing. As you continue to explore and embrace your neurodiverse identity, use the tools and strategies we've discussed to navigate challenges and celebrate your unique contributions to the world. Continuous growth is not just a goal but a way of life. Challenge societal norms, redefine success on your terms, and pursue lifelong learning and adaptation in both personal and professional realms.

Please take the understanding you've obtained and execute self-advocacy strategies, participate in encouraging neighborhoods, and establish and pursue individual objectives. Look for or construct areas that commemorate neurodiversity, as links and shared experiences are essential in promoting a feeling of coming from and assistance.

Advocating for neurodiversity is an effective method of utilizing your voice and experiences to advertise understanding and approval: difficulty fashions and false impressions regarding autism.

Cultivate a feeling of neighborhood by contacting others who share comparable experiences. With each other, we can develop a world where neurodiversity is commemorated and valued.

As you advance your course, consider how you may utilize your trip and experiences to influence and sustain others, adding favorably to your neighborhoods. Be a light of campaigning for and motivating advertising a tradition of understanding and approval for future generations.

In closing, I express my deepest gratitude for your engagement with this book. Your willingness to join this journey of discovery and growth signifies hope for a future where neurodiversity is accepted and embraced as a vital and enriching component of society. Embrace your unique identity, leverage your strengths, and know that a fulfilling and successful life awaits you beyond labels.

Please do not forget to share these experiences with me and the community by leaving your honest opinion of this book on Amazon, you'll show other people somehow related or interested in ASD where they can find the information they're looking for, and pass their passion on how to achieve success beyond spectrum labels forward. If possible photo or video review is even better.

https://www.amazon.com/review/review-your-purchases/?asin=B0DSCMDVT2

With optimism and profound appreciation for each reader, I look forward to a world where every individual is valued for their unique contributions and neurodiversity is celebrated as a cornerstone of our collective humanity.

References

Adina ABA. (n.d.). The best strategies for fostering autism and empathy. Retrieved from https://www.adinaaba.com/post/autism-and-empathy

Autism Parenting Magazine. (n.d.). Autism and social cues: Understanding the challenges. Retrieved from https://www.autismparentingmagazine.com/autism-and-social-cues/

Autism Society. (n.d.). Creating connections for the autism community. Retrieved from https://autismsociety.org/

Borghesi, F., Simoncini, G., Chirico, A., & Cipresso, P. (2024). In medio stat virtus: Moderate cognitive flexibility as a key to affective flexibility responses in long-term HRV. Sensors, 24(24), 8047.

Department of Labor. (n.d.). Autism. Retrieved from https://www.dol.gov/agencies/odep/program-areas/autism

Ebener, D., Fioramonti, D., & Smedema, S. (2016). Career development in men with disabilities: A psychosocial perspective. Career Planning and Adult Development Journal, 32(1), 120–129.

Enna. (n.d.). Neurodiversity and career development: Strategies for advancement. Retrieved from https://enna.org/neurodiversity-and-career-development-strategies-for-advancement/

Goldstar Rehabilitation. (n.d.). Uncovering the negative impact of late autism diagnosis. Retrieved from https://www.goldstarrehab.com/parent-resources/negative-effects-of-an-autism-diagnosis-later-in-life#:~:text=Individuals%20diagnosed%20later%20in%20life,to%20those%20diagnosed%20in%20childhood

Harvard Business Review. (2017, May). Neurodiversity is a competitive advantage. Retrieved from https://hbr.org/2017/05/neurodiversity-as-a-competitive-advantage

Kenneth Roberson, PhD. (n.d.). Effective communication skills for adults with autism. Retrieved from https://kennethrobersonphd.com/discover-effective-communication-tools-for-adults-with-autism-asd/

Knowledge Anywhere. (n.d.). 5 strategies for encouraging lifelong learning and continued education. Retrieved from https://knowledgeanywhere.com/articles/five-strategies-for-encouraging-lifelong-learning-and-continued-education/

Marcia Eckerd, PhD. (n.d.). Navigating life goals as an autistic adult: Strategies for success. Retrieved from https://www.marciaeckerd.com/post/navigating-life-goals-as-an-autistic-adult-strategies-for-success

PubMed. (n.d.). Representation of autism in fictional media: A systematic review. Retrieved from https://pubmed.ncbi.nlm.nih.gov/36802826/

Relational Psych. (n.d.). Self-advocacy strategies for neurodivergent adults. Retrieved from https://www.relationalpsych.group/articles/self-advocacy-strategies-for-neurodivergent-adults

Sachs Center. (n.d.). Social anxiety in adults with autism. Retrieved from https://sachscenter.com/social-anxiety-in-adults-with-autism/#:~:text=It%20is%20essential%20to%20know,in%20dealing%20with%20social%20anxiety

Workvivo. (n.d.). 6 ways to create an autism-inclusive workplace. Retrieved from https://www.workvivo.com/es/blog/six-ways-to-create-an-autism-inclusive-workplace/

Xceptional Academy. (n.d.). 5 autistic professionals share their networking tips. Retrieved from https://xceptionalacademy.org.au/5-autistic-professionals-share-networking-tips/#:~:text=I%20try%20to%20find%20a,those%20are%20my%20go%2Dtos

www.ingramcontent.com/pod-product-compliance
Lightning Source LLC
LaVergne TN
LVHW022054200926
848481LV00003B/909